THE REAL READER'S QUAR

Slightly Foxed

'Curiouser and Curiouser'

NO.47   AUTUMN 2015

Editors Gail Pirkis and Hazel Wood
Marketing and publicity Stephanie Allen and Jennie Paterson
Subscriptions Alarys Gibson, Anna Kirk and Olivia Wilson

Cover illustration: Gail Brodholt, *Autumn*, linocut print

Gail Brodholt is a painter and linocut printmaker of the contemporary urban landscape. Much of her work depicts the London transport network and the journeys made across the city on tubes and trains. She is a Fellow of the Royal Society of Painter-Printmakers and a recipient of many awards and prizes. She works full-time from her studio in Woolwich, South London. To see more of her work visit her website: www.gailbrodholt.com.

Design by Octavius Murray

Layout by Andrew Evans

Colophon and tailpiece by David Eccles

Published by Slightly Foxed Limited
53 Hoxton Square
London N1 6PB

tel 020 7033 0258
fax 0870 1991245
e-mail all@foxedquarterly.com
www.foxedquarterly.com

Slightly Foxed is published quarterly in early March, June, September and December

Printed edition: annual subscription rates (4 issues)
UK £40; Europe £48; Rest of the World £52
Printed edition & digital edition: annual subscription rates
(4 issues plus digital access to all back issues)
UK £50; Europe £58; Rest of the World £62

Single copies of this issue can be bought for £10 (UK), £12 (Europe) or £13 (Rest of the World)

All back issues are also available: for details please ring 020 7033 0258 or visit our website
www.foxedquarterly.com

ISBN 978-1-906562-79-3
ISSN 1742-5794

Printed and bound by Smith Settle, Yeadon, West Yorkshire

Contents

Contents

Llewellyn Thomas,
wood engraving

Our bookshop can obtain any of the books mentioned in this issue.
Slightly Foxed on Gloucester Road, 123 Gloucester Road
London SW7 4TE
enquiries@foxedbooks.com · tel 020 7370 3503

From the Editors

It's hard to believe autumn is here already. But the days are shortening, the air is growing brisker, and gradually the city is coming to life again as people trickle back after the long summer break. London is back in business, and it's all go here in the *Slightly Foxed* office, with the latest of the Slightly Foxed Editions and Slightly Foxed Cubs arriving from the printers, and some new projects afoot.

We've always loved bookplates and featured some in our early issues. Bookplates have a long history, dating from the Middle Ages, when a book was a rare and precious object and the bookplate – usually a fairly simple woodcut – was its owner's identifying mark. Later, copper engraving became popular. Great German artists such as Dürer, Cranach and Holbein all designed bookplates, some very large and elaborate.

In England a great advance in bookplate design came with the invention of the line-block in the nineteenth century and the twentieth-century revival in wood engraving. More, and more varied, people were owning books, and the approach to bookplates became freer and more personal. Distinguished artists like Eric Gill, Joan Hassall and Reynolds Stone created bookplates inspired by an individual's character rather than his coat of arms. This tradition is continued by many of the finest English wood engravers, such as our own contributor Simon Brett. Not only is a bookplate a practical way of keeping track of one's books but it gives the book itself a special interest, identity and provenance.

Commissioning an original bookplate, however, is a costly business, and this gave us the idea of producing a more affordable bookplate which would still be elegant and personal. So we're offering readers the opportunity to acquire a bookplate featuring a wood engraving by one of our favourite engravers, Howard Phipps. There are four charming scenes to choose from, with a space on which the individual reader's name will be printed. You can see the images on p.95 and read more in the enclosed leaflet, where you will also find details of this year's Slightly Foxed Christmas card, and our 2016 calendar.

As to other news, we can't resist mentioning the latest Slightly Foxed Edition, the writer and naturalist Gavin Maxwell's childhood memoir *The House of Elrig* (see p. 12). It is an extraordinarily powerful book which tells the story of a sensitive small boy, entirely at one with the wild moorland countryside of the great Scottish estate on which he grows up, who is wrenched from this paradise to go to a series of brutalizing English schools. It is also a wryly observed and often comic picture of the philistine life of the Edwardian upper class, and of his own grand and eccentric family.

There are also two new additions to Ronald Welch's splendid Carey family series (see p.39), both written with the verve and incredible attention to detail that make the books so exceptional. *Escape from France* sees young Richard Carey dispatched by his father to help the Careys' aristocratic relatives escape revolutionary France, while in *Nicholas Carey* the series reaches the Crimean War, in which young Captain Nicholas Carey experiences the horror of a Crimean winter and distinguishes himself at the battles of Sebastopol and The Redan.

Finally, a small reminder about Readers' Day. It's on Saturday 7 November at our usual haunt, the Art Workers' Guild in Bloomsbury, and we have an excellent and varied line-up of speakers this year. We've still a few tickets left, so do contact the office if you're interested. We look forward very much to seeing you at what has now become a regular *SF* 'family' event.

GAIL PIRKIS & HAZEL WOOD

Curiouser and Curiouser

BRANDON ROBSHAW

A man is driving home at night, somewhere in the West Midlands. He gets lost in a sprawling, anonymous suburb, and his car is low on petrol. Then he chances upon a hotel where he is welcomed in and shown to the dining-room. The place is uncomfortably hot, with thick carpets and curtains. He is served a huge bowl of thick soup followed by an enormous bowl of macaroni cheese, and after that a gigantic pile of turkey accompanied by five different vegetables. When he is unable to finish it, the waitress responds by flying into a rage and flinging his plate to the floor. The manager appears to smooth things over – and as the man is led from the dining-room, he observes that one of the diners has his ankle fettered to an iron rail under the table . . .

Welcome to the strange world of Robert Aickman (this story, 'The Hospice', goes on to get much stranger). I first encountered his work as a teenager in the 1970s, when I discovered the *Fontana Book of Great Ghost Stories*; Aickman edited the first eight volumes of this series, writing the introduction to each one and usually including one of his own stories. His selections formed a marvellous introduction to the ghost-story canon with tales by J. Sheridan Le Fanu, L. P. Hartley, Ambrose Bierce, M. R. James, Saki, Oliver Onions and Edgar Allan Poe among others. Yet Robert Aickman's own stories

Robert Aickman, *Dark Entries* (256pp · £7.99 · ISBN 9780571311774); *Cold Hand in Mine* (368pp · £8.99 · ISBN 9780571311743); *The Unsettled Dust* (384pp · £8.99 · ISBN 9780571311736); and *The Wine-Dark Sea* (464pp · £8.99 · ISBN 9780571311729) are all available as Faber paperbacks.

were always among the best, and unlike anyone else's. It wasn't always clear that they *were* ghost stories; in fact he himself preferred the term 'strange stories', and I can't think of a better label.

Then, in the late Seventies, I was browsing in my local library and came upon a volume of his stories, *Cold Hand in Mine* (and isn't that a brilliant title?). It gave me a peculiar sense of satisfaction to see that he existed outside the Fontana series. There were eight stories included, five of which I had never seen before. I took it home and devoured it.

All of Aickman's tales (he wrote 48 in all) include some kind of supernatural element. 'Pages from a Young Girl's Journal' is a vampire story, 'Ringing the Changes' is a zombie story, others feature ghostly visitants of various kinds. But that in itself is not what is strange about them. The characters are strange. The events are strange. The scenarios are strange. It's hard to convey the special, unsettling atmosphere of Aickman's work to anyone who isn't acquainted with it; but let me try.

His stories tend to centre on a protagonist who is a loner, somewhat detached from the world, often rather a fussy, finicky person who stumbles upon some weird set-up involving dubious, mysterious and not-quite-human people. In 'The Swords', for example, a young travelling salesman comes across a seedy little fair in Wolverhampton. Inside a tent is a young woman sitting on a chair on a stage. Beside her is a pile of swords, 'stacked criss-cross like cheese straws'. The men in the tent take it in turns to kiss her and then drive a sword into her body. Which draws no blood. The protagonist leaves hastily before it's his turn; but later he encounters the girl and her manager in town and they offer him a private show . . .

Or there's 'The Cicerones', featuring a tourist, Trant, who visits a cathedral in Belgium. The cathedral is nearly empty. Trant looks at various gruesome depictions of martyrdoms in side-chapels. He sees a terrifying-looking figure standing in the pulpit, which turns out to be an optical illusion; another visitor laughs with him about it, then says 'Holy, holy, holy' (Trant is *almost* sure that's what he said) and wanders off. An American tourist with a peculiar manner appears and makes some enigmatic comments about martyrdom. Then an odd, self-possessed child appears and offers to take Trant to the crypt . . .

Certain motifs recur: several stories feature odd, knowing children, whose sex can't easily be determined. Strangers appear and are either oddly talkative or oddly silent. Fog, mist, twilight and overcast skies feature strongly, as do dim yellow lights glimmering from windows. So do sounds heard from other rooms: full-on screams and shrieks, or sometimes more ambiguous noises.

Aickman uses a wide variety of settings – an island in Finland, a flat in a London square, a village in Northamptonshire, a tour through eighteenth-century Italy – and in all of them he vividly conveys the sheer physicality of the place: the weather, the light, the texture and feel of surfaces, the furnishings of houses or the configuration of natural features. And there is a heavy emphasis on the banal, the ordinariness of things, which makes the strangeness feel even stranger. The swords, for example, in the story of that name have nothing gleaming or glamorous about them: 'The blades were a dull grey, and the hilts were made of some black stuff, possibly plastic. They looked thoroughly mass-produced and industrial.'

Events in Aickman's stories are entirely unpredictable; yet when they occur, one feels they were somehow inevitable. One simple but effective trick he often uses is to describe something slightly strange – someone's unconventional appearance, an unexplained noise – and then observe that the main character was 'badly frightened'. But why? You begin to feel uneasy yourself. Did you miss something? And as the story proceeds, of course, you realize that the character was quite right to be frightened; in fact they weren't frightened enough. There are gaps in the narrative, leaving the reader to piece together the full horror. The endings are frequently inconclusive, leaving one with a sense that there is an explanation just out of reach. Aickman's characters don't usually come to sticky ends, though sometimes they do. More often they survive, but are psychologically damaged by their experiences.

Aickman has a distinctive writing style: precise, mannered, even pedantic. There are touches of erudition – the occasional Latin tag, allusions to art and music, references to Shakespeare, Goethe, Homer, epigraphs from Strindberg or Céline. If all this makes him sound a stuffy writer, well, he's not. His stories are long – often near-novella length – but compulsively readable. Commit to the first page of a Robert Aickman story and you are pulled, *dragged* into it.

One gets a strong sense of a personality, and indeed his real-life character seems to have been not too different from his literary persona. Like many of his protagonists, he seems to have been something of a loner; certainly not without friends, but he saw them on his own terms, when he wished, and seldom allowed them to meet one another.

Four collections of his strange stories were brought out by Faber in 2014 to commemorate the centenary of his birth – *Dark Entries, Cold Hand in Mine, The Unsettled Dust* and *The Wine-Dark Sea* – and each includes an afterword by a close friend. All agree that although he could be extremely charming he could also be very difficult. There was undoubtedly something aloof and élitist about him: in one of his Fontana introductions he bemoans the increasing uniformity and social equality of the modern world. One of his characters, in the story 'Meeting Mr Millar', observes that 'change of its nature is for the worse'. It was no doubt his love of the past that drove his work as a conservationist; he was one of the founder-members of the Inland Waterways Association and was an effective and energetic campaigner, though, characteristically, he later fell out with his co-founder, Tom Rolt.

One of his favourite pastimes with friends was to read aloud his latest stories – which, considering that some of them are as many as 70 pages long, might be thought to be pushing the claims of friendship a bit far. His first book, published in 1951, was a collection of stories with Elizabeth Jane Howard. They had a brief relationship, which Elizabeth ended; Aickman seems never to have got over this. He kept a photo of her by his bed; and many years later, when he knew she was coming to visit him as he lay dying, he asked to be shaved so he could look smart for her. He died in 1981, having refused conventional treatment for cancer and opted for homeopathy instead.

I don't know whether I would have liked him as a person, and I am fairly sure he would not have liked me; but it was his difficult, proud, prickly, fastidious, solitary nature that enabled him to produce these marvellously strange stories. During his lifetime his writing was highly regarded by the literary establishment but was not widely known outside it. He certainly never made much money, probably because of his uncompromising refusal to write more commercially. But his writing has endured and his reputation is growing.

It's not easy to find literary comparisons for his work. The obvious one would be with the great writer of ghost stories M. R. James: both are erudite, both are skilled at creating atmosphere and supplying the telling scary detail. But Aickman was annoyed by the comparison. In his introduction to *The Fourth Fontana Book of Great Ghost Stories* he argued that there was an off-putting, donnish detachment in James's storytelling (although he exempted 'A School Story' and included it in the volume). Certainly Aickman writes *through* his characters, not *about* them as James did, and his stories are of a very different kind. A closer comparison might be with Franz Kafka, whose dreamlike logic Aickman's writing shares. But really Aickman's work is *sui generis*. If you don't know his strange stories, you must try them. And if you do, they bear rereading exceptionally well.

BRANDON ROBSHAW is a lecturer in Creative Writing and Children's Literature at the Open University. He is also a children's author, though his latest novel, *The Big Wish* (2015), is not as strange a story as some of Aickman's.

Mowgli with a Gun

GALEN O'HANLON

A few months before his thirteenth birthday, the young and miserable Gavin Maxwell crept out of St Wulfric's prep school to send a 'thoroughly hysterical' letter to his mother. At the end of it he wrote, 'For God's sake take me away from this awful place.' She answered his plea, and he was whisked away in the middle of the Spring term, 'a quaking jelly of misery and self-pity'. He went straight home, to the House of Elrig – the house he grew up in on the edge of the vast Monreith estate in Galloway, surrounded by woods and peat bogs and heather.

I was also a quaking jelly at school. I would long for the holidays, when we would pack up and drive to Scotland, to be dragged through ever thicker rain in search of ever rarer birds. My friends saw the sun in August. I saw the Shetland wren. So I find Maxwell's books deeply comforting: none more so than *The House of Elrig* (1965), which describes in lucid detail the impossible social awkwardness of school, and the irresistible freedom of the natural world.

The childhood he describes in this memoir is at once strange and totally familiar: there are trees to be climbed, things to be learnt, and games to be played. But there are also governesses, shooting parties and an Uncle Percy – or rather, *the* Uncle Percy, Duke of Northumberland. It takes place between the wars: Maxwell was born in 1914, three months before his father was killed at Antwerp.

The House of Elrig covers his first sixteen years, moving through his earliest memories and blissful days at home to his patchy school career, which ends quite suddenly with a rare and near-fatal illness that has him bedridden on his sixteenth birthday. He'd snuck out of the dormitory at dawn that day, to go rabbit shooting:

> A dull grey dawn with the dew sopping on deep summer grass and nettles. Everything smelled wet and green, and the air was intimate with the calling of jackdaws awakening from their hollow oaks and Palladian ruins.

Instantly familiar to anyone who's woken up early to the smell of dawn in July; strange, perhaps, for the Palladian ruins. But this is Stowe, Maxwell's public school, where even the jackdaws are well accommodated. He and his accomplice shoot a rabbit, and he takes enormous satisfaction from the discovery that the other boy doesn't know how to gut it: 'I showed him, expertly and with contempt.' And there you have Maxwell's skill in autobiography: capturing not only the events of his childhood, but also the emotions and mindset of his younger self.

The House of Elrig begins with a journey home, and Maxwell's easy, captivating style is immediately apparent. We see the house in the first line, although it's not particularly welcoming: a 'gaunt, grey stone building on a hillside of heather and bracken'. It's almost unreachable, sitting at the end of a road in a stark landscape of coarse grass, bracken and stunted trees whose heads 'seem to be forever bowed and straining towards the land'. It's not in Elrig itself, but on the very edge of the habitable world, and beyond it stretches 'the untamed land of peat-bog and heathery hills, of sphagnum moss and myrtle and waving bog cotton'. The prose is thick with the detail of a landscape that might be wild and unforgiving but is nevertheless full of life. The bog is 'sweet with the haunting trilling of curlews and the wild notes of tumbling lapwings', and there, in the centre of it, is the boy Maxwell:

> After a shower of rain the air smells of the bog myrtle, and big
> black slugs come out on the edges of the untrammelled road.
> I walk home at the opposite side of the road from my nurse;
> my mother, watching from distant windows of the house,
> worries that we have quarrelled, but we are counting slugs in
> competition.

It is beguiling, and instantly appealing – he delves into the broad
magic of a landscape, only to home in on a tiny, everyday detail: the
slugs. In this style of subtle humour and intricate detail he explores
his childhood, the origins of his interest in the natural world, and
his penchant for collecting unusual pets.

Maxwell made his name with a pet otter, of course – but the otters
came later. In *The House of Elrig* we see his early impulse to domes-
ticate whatever wild beasts happen to fall into his lap. His sister has
a series of goats, which behave like 'reasonably well-behaved dogs'
when the children take them on long walks – only displaying their
goatishness with skittish avoidance of recapture, 'and occasionally
munching on a pocket-handkerchief'. Then there are the more outlandish pets: a family of rooks, several hedgehogs ('disappointing'), a
pet jackdaw and a heron.

Maxwell's fondest memories are of Andrew, the owl. He plucked
him from the nest as a little puffball when he was out hunting for
birds' eggs one day. Andrew grew to be quite affectionate, and would
ride the handlebars of their bicycles, perch on their shoulders and
come to their call – 'sweeping down from the leafy gloom of some
great tree'. And then, in a sudden and devastating tragedy of the natural world meeting the human, the owl is battered to death with a
stick when, 'in our absence at school, he alighted on the push handle
of a pram belonging to a stranger, who believed the bird to be attack-
ing the baby'.

This seems to foreshadow the horrifying scene in *Ring of Bright
Water*, in which a malicious neighbour kills Maxwell's pet otter

Mijbil. Maxwell became famous for that book: it's one of the bestselling nature books of all time. It inspired a whole generation of naturalists, and played a significant part in the birth of conservationism. And in *The House of Elrig* we see where it all began.

Leaving aside the death of his animals, Maxwell's pre-school childhood was a happy, isolated one, spent in the company of his three siblings, his mother and a long line of governesses. He had a parade of aunts as eccentric as anyone on the outskirts of the aristocracy could wish for, but one of them, Aunt Moo, was also a serious research zoologist. It was she who ignited Maxwell's passion for the natural world – showing him the excitement of ponds and rock pools, and also the hours of joy to be found in discovering the inhabitants of every square yard of the garden.

The House of Elrig divides very clearly into Maxwell's childhood at school and his childhood at home. Indeed, the two 'were so utterly unrelated that it seems now as if they must have run parallel in time and been lived by two different people':

> I used to think of life like telegraph wires watched from a train window – in the holidays they would soar up until it seemed they would climb the sky, only to be inevitably slapped down by the next telegraph post – the term.

Until he went to school he had never met anyone his own age – he had no idea how to function in a group of aggressive schoolboys, and the process of making a friend baffled him. The masters made it worse by emphasizing his status as a minor aristocrat, giving his peers all the more reason to single him out. But amidst all the misery – the beatings, the pinched buttocks, the boxing – there were occasional flashes of interest. Mr Sillar taught drawing and geography, and was a devoted naturalist. Just before Maxwell's abrupt exit from

St Wulfric's, Mr Sillar tells him that 'no one can understand complicated things like their own lives and other people unless they understand simple things like animals and birds'.

For Maxwell, school was an alien place of unfathomable social rituals. So once he had escaped the torment of St Wulfric's for good, he eliminated the memory of it from his mind, and returned to the sort of education he was used to:

> [Spending] long days with Hannam the gamekeeper as he went the rounds of his distant traps, close at his heels as a shadow while with the wisdom of a lifetime he outwitted birds and beasts classified by his rules as vermin, listening to the low rumble of his voice as, sheltering behind a stone dyke from some blinding hill shower, he would try to impart to me his intimate knowledge of wild life.

These days at home with the gamekeeper rehabilitate him. Hannam is the sort of father figure that Maxwell had always lacked; showing him the deep pleasure of long days in the woods, on the hills, and by the fire at the end of the day. Then his brother returns from school for the Spring holidays, and they are back to their usual routine:

> The perilous climbing of an infinity of trees . . . the thorny, tweed-tearing grip of hawthorn trees with the basket of a magpie's nest at the top; the raw red bark of a great Scots pine into which the bite of shoe-strapped climbing-irons was as satisfying as the crunch of a biscuit; the slow, cautious, often terrifying descent carrying the plundered eggs in the peak of a tweed cap. Whatever it was, and no matter how much blood was drawn, it was home.

This is Maxwell's prose in full flow – and it is what makes the book so captivating. He moves from the very large to the very small, from the infinity of trees to the crunch of his boot against the bark of the Scots pine, from the giddying descent to the neat, snuggled eggs in a tweed cap. He builds rhythm in the semicolons, links the general to the particular, flows from one image to the next and the next until, with the satisfying clunk of a natural close, he comes home.

It is a brief hiatus, but it's a turning-point. His next prep school is much better, and when he goes to Stowe, he begins finally to fit in. Stoics are allowed to keep dogs, and there is a relaxed attitude towards education, although not so relaxed as to allow rabbit-shooting before breakfast. The other boys don't mind as much when faced with how different he is, and he is accepted, a little awkwardly, as 'a sort of Mowgli with a gun'.

Then comes the illness, and he is trapped for months in various sickbeds along the south coast – unable to travel far, cut off from the one place he wants to be: Elrig. When he finally makes it home in the last few pages, we share his sense of freedom and release. This is a beautiful, sparkling book, a brief glimpse of a wild childhood that is recognizable even in its strangeness – he has captured the essence of youth, that delicate balance of happiness and misery.

GALEN O'HANLON lives in Glasgow, where he writes, cycles and dreams of having an owl called Andrew to sit on his handlebars.

Gavin Maxwell's *The House of Elrig* (256pp) is now available from Slightly Foxed in a new limited and numbered cloth-bound pocket edition of 2,000 copies, each priced at £16 (UK), £18 (Europe) or £19 (Rest of the World). All prices include post and packing. Copies may be ordered by post (53 Hoxton Square, London N1 6PB), by phone (020 7033 0258) or via our website www.foxedquarterly.com.

Romance in Broadmoor

MAGGIE FERGUSSON

It's odd to feel nostalgia for a place you've never set foot in, but that's what I feel for Broadmoor. In my imagination, I can pass through the main gate into the maze of red-brick Victorian buildings, cross the courtyard and walk down the long corridors of the men's and women's wings. I can turn the heavy brass doorknob and step into the office of the chief medical superintendent, with its huge desk and its watercolours by Richard Dadd, the gifted artist who, in 1843, murdered his father, believing him to be the Devil. And in my memory I can still hear the siren – plangent, baleful – whining through the Home Counties mist.

Since its foundation in 1863, Broadmoor has been home to the most dangerous criminal lunatics in Britain – Ronnie Kray and Peter Sutcliffe, for example – and many assume that it must therefore be situated on some blasted heath, miles from civilization. In fact, it's in Berkshire, a stone's throw from several institutions of rather different kinds. It used to be said that you could be educated at Wellington College, pass out of the military college at Sandhurst and end your days in Broadmoor without travelling more than a mile or so in any direction. I grew up and went to school in Ascot, and Broadmoor was a looming though invisible presence for my siblings and me, lending a thrilling frisson to the safe monotony of our suburban childhood.

The siren was tested weekly, so when we heard it on a Monday

Patrick McGrath, *Asylum* (1996)
Penguin · Pb · 256pp · £9.99 · ISBN 9780140258226

morning it was, despite its mournful tone, reassuring: '10 o'clock, and all's well'. But very occasionally the banshee wail struck up at another time of the day or week, and then we knew that some crazed villain was on the loose. And of course we half-hoped that he or she was heading straight for us.

I first remember this happening during evening study in the autumn term, just after I started at my secondary school. Tradition had it that an escaped Broadmoor patient had once made a beeline for St Mary's Convent, Ascot, so in a well-practised drill the nuns pinned up the outer skirts of their habits and set off to patrol the grounds, armed with hockey sticks. Reverend Mother, meantime, visited the junior school to give us a pep talk. If we happened to meet a 'gentleman' on the way back through the rhododendrons for supper, she said, we must be sure to engage him in conversation. 'You should say something perfectly natural, like, "Are you a caddy from the golf course?"'

Schools nowadays pride themselves on keeping teenagers permanently stretched and occupied, but things were different in the early 1970s. We were bored; and Broadmoor inspired a dreadful fascination. What was life there like (could it be odder than ours in the convent)? Were the men and women obvious, raving lunatics, or were they calm-seeming and crafty? And how was madness defined and diagnosed? Ian Brady and Myra Hindley had committed the Moors murders in tandem; yet one was in an asylum, the other in prison. Why?

None of these questions was answered, and as I grew up and moved away from home – and out of earshot of the siren – they faded. But they didn't entirely disappear, and over lunch one day in the autumn of 1996, I mentioned my fascination with Broadmoor to the novelist David Hughes. Had I read Patrick McGrath's *Asylum*, he asked in response. No? I *must!* McGrath had grown up at Broadmoor, where his father had been appointed medical superintendent in 1957; and, though his fictional asylum wasn't named, there was little doubt that it was based on his childhood home. The novel was just out, and getting rave reviews. I bought it immediately.

Asylum will be a treat in store for some, so I'm reluctant to give away too much of the plot. But, in broad outline, it revolves around a catastrophic affair between Stella Raphael, the beautiful, wayward wife of the deputy superintendent of a high-security mental asylum, and Edgar Stark, a psychiatric patient of 'restless, devious intelligence' and powerful sexual magnetism. Stark has been hospitalized for treatment after murdering and decapitating his wife, and then removing her eyes. When he joins a working party of patients to refurbish the dilapidated greenhouse in the Raphaels' garden, Stella meets him and falls fatally in love.

The opening pages of the novel transport us back to the long, hot summer of 1959. With all the brilliance of E. M. Forster in *A Passage to India*, L. P. Hartley in *The Go-Between* or Scott Fitzgerald in *The Great Gatsby*, McGrath makes us swelter in the relentless, mind-bending heat. 'The trees hanging over the garden walls seemed weighted with a peculiar dull heaviness . . . the grass in the meadow thick and high and the climbing roses blowsy in their second flush . . .' In Stella Raphael, reason and inhibition evaporate. Caution is thrown to the hot wind.

We are planted in an era, as well as a season – an era tantalizing to me for being just outside the scope of my own memory. It's evoked in powder compacts and headscarves, cigarettes and endless G&Ts, but above all in the languid, dragging days of its married women. Today, Stella Raphael might be 'stressed'; in 1959, she's just bored. Her husband, Max, has provided her with a safe haven after a rackety Foreign Office childhood. He's kind and decent, but lacking in moral or physical imagination; he channels his limited libido into his work. Edgar Stark, by contrast, makes Stella feel 'bold, original, free'. Into her predictable middle-class life he injects a shot of high risk, and it thrills her.

As the tension rises, and Stella seems to be speeding headlong towards the same gruesome end as Edgar Stark's wife, it would have been easy for McGrath to slide into melodrama. But the novel is narrated not by Stella or Max or Edgar, but by Dr Cleave, a forensic psychiatrist regarded by all three parties as an ally. Cleave's tone is cool, unruffled, judicious: it keeps the horror controlled, and so heightens it. Only very gradually does one begin to suspect that Peter Cleave is the most sinister character of the piece.

And so, amidst the compulsive, page-turning drama, big questions are introduced. Where do the borders between sanity and madness lie? And does the practice of psychiatry have a particular appeal for those who need to demonstrate their own mental stability? The biographer Victoria Glendinning began her working life as a psychiatric social worker in a 1,500-bed mental hospital. She remembers seeing a group of psychiatrists advancing down one of the long corridors. The shambling patients flattened themselves against the walls as the medics sped by, laughing and chatting loudly, white coats flying. They were 'getting off' (her words) on the weakness and inadequacy of others. They might have been a fleet of Peter Cleaves.

I turned the last page of *Asylum* with a sense of double satisfaction: it's a brilliant novel, and it had brought me as close to the real Broadmoor, surely, as I would ever get. But chance is a fine thing. A couple of years ago, I started working for *The Economist*'s bi-monthly magazine *Intelligent Life*. One of my jobs there is to commission pieces of memoir. When I Googled 'Broadmoor', I saw that its 150th anniversary was approaching. Then I tracked down Patrick McGrath in New York. No, he said – other than fictionally, he had never written about his childhood; and yes, this felt like a good moment to try.

What landed in my inbox a month later was one of the most absorbing pieces I've ever read. It was filled with the kind of detail we hungered for as schoolgirls: descriptions of life in 'Block 6', where the most disturbed male patients were housed; memories of the escape of Frank Mitchell, a member of the Kray gang, in the summer of 1958 (after he was caught, the Broadmoor children lined the route to watch his return in a Black Maria). Ian Brady, it turned out, had never been in Broadmoor: he was one of two men whom Dr McGrath considered not ill but evil, and refused to admit.

Paragraph by paragraph, it became clear just how much of *Asylum* was rooted in truth. As a boy, eavesdropping on staff dinner parties, Patrick McGrath learned that a doctor's wife had been 'compromised' by a patient sent to work in her garden, and that a female patient had, after dark, scooped out her own eyes with a teaspoon. 'Kentigern', the McGraths' family home – a draughty Victorian villa 110 yards from the main gate, composed of large, impossible-to-heat rooms and set in rambling acres of lawns and rhododendrons – was the same house Max and Stella Raphael move into at the beginning of the novel. And there really were what I had assumed to be fictional doctor-patient dances, ahead of which female patients made themselves up from 'an old biscuit tin filled with a clutter of lipsticks and eye pencils, little vials of perfume, jars of cream and powder, all donated by members of staff'.

Yet, more even than the detail of the piece, I was moved by its atmosphere. Patrick McGrath was too young, when his family moved to Broadmoor, to understand that others might think it a strange place to grow up. He passed his childhood 'in happy ignorance of it all'. And he loved it. The vast grounds, with their woods and cricket pitch, were paradise for a small boy. The patients in yellow corduroys and donkey jackets, who built his swing and played football with him, were his first, firm friends. He looks back on it all with longing. If there's one word that describes the tone of his piece, the word is 'nostalgic'.

MAGGIE FERGUSSON is Director of the Royal Society of Literature and the author of a prize-winning biography of George Mackay Brown. On the publication of the latter her daughters made her swear she would never write another book.

An Unexpected Gift

JULIAN HOFFMAN

A friend of mine likes to send me souvenirs from his travels. We share a love of odd postcards, and occasionally I find in my letterbox a picture of a curiously empty parking lot or an industrial unit on the outskirts of a town. We also have a mutual affection for Turkish coffee and the subtle variations in the way in which it's roasted and served in different parts of the Balkans, North Africa and the Middle East, so my post sometimes carries the strong, aromatic scent of a new discovery, though the rich, cardamom-flavoured variety he once sent me from a Palestinian shop in Jerusalem remains unsurpassed to this day. So when a slim padded envelope arrived from him last year I was expecting something similar – a memento from the road. Instead the envelope contained a gift that sent *me* on a journey.

I'm continually amazed by how many remarkable writers can pass you by, even when you think you read a lot. My friend had sent me a copy of *The Cone-Gatherers* (1955) by Robin Jenkins. I'd never heard of him, but I later discovered that in his long life (1912–2005) he'd written thirty novels and two short-story collections. His books have also appeared on the school syllabus in his native Scotland, and the Robin Jenkins Award was established to recognize exceptional works of environmental literature. But I didn't know any of this when I sat down to read the book.

The Cone-Gatherers is set on a Scottish estate beside a sea loch during the Second World War. While her husband is away fighting,

Robin Jenkins, *The Cone-Gatherers* (1955)
Canongate · Pb · 240pp · £9.99 · ISBN 9780857862350

Lady Runcie-Campbell is in sole charge of the estate, and she has grudgingly allowed two brothers to work in her woodland following an appeal by a forestry officer on the grounds of patriotism.

The two brothers, Calum and Neil, have been given the job of harvesting the cones of the trees for seed, and it is in the woods of this extensive estate – actually in the trees themselves – that we first meet them. Calum is 31, a hunchback and simple-minded, but also as 'indigenous as squirrel or bird'. In the book's dreamlike opening, chaffinches flutter about him while he works at the top of a larch, nearer to the sky than the ground. He's a man who releases rabbits from the gamekeeper's snares and who feels an instinctive connection with the sentient and suffering world around him.

Calum's older brother, Neil, is both troubled and delighted by this compassionate innocence, knowing how exposed and vulnerable it leaves them in a world at war and with little time for sentiment. Duror, the gamekeeper of the estate, repelled by Calum's physical deformity and his tender empathy with animals, vows to destroy the brothers for polluting the 'sanctuary' of his woods. His dark malevolence is a constant, troubling presence for the two brothers, a shadow of the not-so-distant conflict.

The brothers are outsiders on the estate in more ways than one. Sent to harvest cones on their own, they've had to leave behind their familiar community of fellow foresters. During their stay they are housed in a dingy, leaking shack, while the palatial stone manor of the landowners is clearly visible from high in the trees where they work. Since their mother died soon after Calum's birth and they never knew their father, Neil has become his younger brother's devoted guardian – a role which has prevented him from marrying or enlisting in the army. So they have joined the ranks of the men on the home front – the elderly, the young, the ill and the unwilling.

Robin Jenkins was himself a conscientious objector during the war, and was sent to work for the Forestry Commission in Argyll. His wartime experiences there helped shape a novel that is both moving and richly symbolic, a portrait of two siblings on their own in the world, making the most of what little they've been given.

At the core of the book is a searing portrayal of social injustice. Although I was born in England, I moved to Canada with my parents when I was young and grew up without an inkling of the class system they had left behind. But years later, when I eventually returned, I was startled to see how thoroughly class still permeated British society. The corrupted consequences of entitlement by birth are personified by Lady Runcie-Campbell when she observes: 'These cone-gatherers, for instance. Obviously, in any way you like to look at it, they are our inferiors; they would be the first to admit it themselves; it is self-evident . . . The maintenance of society on a civilized basis depends on us.'

Kathleen Lindsley, 'April Snow Showers' wood engraving

In his spare time, Calum carves rabbits and squirrels from pieces of wood. He doesn't question his position in life, longing only to be free with the birds in the trees. It is Neil who carries the anguish and burden of their humiliation. 'Aren't the kennels at the house bigger than our hut?' he asks his brother. 'We're human beings just like them. We need space to live and breathe in.'

As tensions begin to rise on the estate, and the gamekeeper's violent, brooding menace grows, the brothers use a free Saturday afternoon to leave the estate and travel into town where another side of their lives is revealed. There they are warmly welcomed by everyone they meet, receiving the largest portions of fish and chips at the café and extra rations from beneath the counter at the grocer's. While a war is being fought on the continent, and on the estate a class conflict is unfolding which will affect the future of everyone caught up in it, Jenkins celebrates such small moments of empathy and connection in the fleeting human lives he sketches. This luminous tenderness at the heart of the novel is captivating.

When I first read *The Cone-Gatherers* it was the story of the brothers that lingered with me long after the book's extraordinary last scene. But rereading it recently, I found another strand of the story that now stays with me. Roderick, the heir to the estate, has been raised as a man of 'education, breeding, and discernment' and groomed in all the duties expected of a future baronet. Yet he seeks friendship with the brothers and repudiates the social conventions of his caste. He is the questioning moral centre of this deeply compassionate novel, a boy who instinctively sees the connection between the war being fought overseas and the inherited patterns of injustice being perpetuated on the land that will one day be his. Unlike his mother he admires the hard-working brothers and wants to be at home in the tree-tops beside them, labouring to gather cones for the sake of future green woods and sharing a world in which finches land wondrously in his hands.

Books enter our lives in myriad ways – through reviews and by word of mouth, by accident or serendipity, through remembered conversations or browsing in libraries and bookshops. And then there are those gifts that arrive unannounced. These are the books I especially treasure – those by an author I might never have discovered, that reveal a deeply felt world I would never otherwise have known.

JULIAN HOFFMAN lives in a village in the mountains of northern Greece and is the author of *The Small Heart of Things: Being at Home in a Beckoning World*.

The American Dostoevsky

JUSTIN CARTWRIGHT

I have read so much Updike, so many articles, so many collections of his criticism and journalism, and virtually all his many novels, that I sometimes think I know more about his thought processes than I do about my own.

In his introduction to *The Early Stories, 1953–1975*, John Updike speaks candidly about his professional life. His inspiration, he says, has been drawn from life; he has always believed that 'out there was where I belonged, immersed in the ordinary which careful explication would reveal to be the extraordinary'. And this, I think, gave him the leitmotif of his writing life and made him the writer he became.

He was, consciously, the product of small-town Pennsylvania and always his remarkable mother's son. His father, a schoolteacher, is a rather shadowy figure in his accounts. His mother moved the family from their home town of Shillington out to a farm in the countryside, which Updike described as 'the crucial detachment of my life'. In the late Forties and Fifties he had discovered the joy of films, and he would go to local movie houses as often as possible, experiences which he treasured and described nostalgically. He once wrote a wonderful line: all movies are really the story of two huge faces on a screen coming together and eventually kissing.

For the rest of his life he harked back to Pennsylvania, most

John Updike, *Rabbit, Run* (1960), *Rabbit Redux* (1971), *Rabbit Is Rich* (1980) and *Rabbit at Rest* (1990) are available in a single volume, *Rabbit Angstrom: The Four Novels*: Everyman · Hb · 1,519pp · £25 · ISBN 9781857152142.

obviously for his Rabbit Angstrom novels; he cherished the local idiom, the banality of conversation, the deep-grained, unthinking patriotism, the rumours of adultery, and all the small endeavours and lapses of the people in the towns he knew. He had a great visual awareness too, and many of the towns he appropriated are almost lovingly summoned, even as they are lapsing into neglect and decay.

In his progress from rural Pennsylvania, via Harvard and Oxford, to international celebrity, he never tried to distance himself from his background. In fact he needed it as a kind of emotional base camp, something that he could explore and use. During his year in Oxford he studied drawing at the Ruskin. He had a very intense, almost painterly, appreciation of place, a sensitivity he applied to writing his novels, so that his descriptions of New York, New England and Pennsylvania are rich and precise. He was a wonderful observer of art; over the years he wrote some outstanding art criticism for the *New York Review of Books* and other magazines. His last piece about art appeared in the *New York Times* shortly before he died in 2009. Poignantly it was called 'Always Looking'. The year before he had reviewed the J. M. W. Turner exhibition in Washington with his customary diligence and insight.

He was always an original boy, in his early days obsessed with paper and cartoons rather than the act of writing. He sent off stories and cartoons and they began to be published. He was very young, with a growing family, when he was invited to join the staff of the *New Yorker* in 1954; after two years he retreated from New York to an ordinary town in Massachusetts and he stayed in the area until he died. He was a Yankee, in some ways, in his decency and deliberateness, I thought, despite his background. All his life he loved Harvard and what he had achieved there on the staff of the *Harvard Crimson*, a traditional starting-point for budding Harvard writers.

I have more or less worshipped Updike since I first read his short story 'Pigeon Feathers', long before I came from South Africa to England and Oxford. Some years ago I went to Boston to interview him and we spent what he described as 'a beguiling three hours'. It is there, in one of his books I asked him to sign. I am not sure I beguiled him, but he certainly beguiled me. He had deeply ingrained good manners, old-fashioned manners. When we met at a very grand hotel in Boston, he was concerned that I was not wearing a tie; he thought it was obligatory, but I had checked and I told him

so. He smiled wanly; it was a small insight, I thought, into both his parochialism and the extent of his Yankee sensibility.

In my study, I keep a photograph of him that I took at our first meeting, and his gentle, knowing smile is warming. He had a large nose, which gave him the appearance of the prow of a boat. When we talked he seemed surprised that I knew his books so well, and particularly surprised that I had read *The Coup* (1978). This little-known book is set in tropical Africa – Updike had half-African grandchildren – and it is an astonishing piece of work. He told me that day that the only excuse for reading is to steal, so I felt able to tell him that my first serious novel, *Interior*, owed a lot to *The Coup*.

What is particularly astonishing about *The Coup* is that it is not about a world Updike knew well, yet it has a beautiful and imaginative lyricism and an unforgettable inventiveness which give the lie to the theory that he could only write what he saw. *The Coup* suggests to me that, had he wanted to, he could have had another, quite different career. And perhaps it would have been different if he had not struck a rich vein with the Tarbox novels, set on the beaches and in the houses of the young and adulterous of Massachusetts. One novel alone, *Couples*, published in 1968, earned him more than $1 million, a huge amount back then. It was almost scandalously explicit, and of course avidly read. I once asked him about the difficulties of writing about sex and he said that as a writer you have to apply the same standards to all sections of a novel: you can't restrict yourself by cutting away to agitated palm trees or suggestive waves crashing on a beach.

He was, in his own way, religious; in his short story 'The Deacon' you get the strong sense that for Updike – as for the deacon himself – faith is the persistence and continuity of humanity, possibly inseparable. His faith was also a kind of pantheism: God could be found in the architecture of churches and in the persistence of habit. In 'The Deacon' his description of Miles, who opens the church door to find that there are no worshippers, is very moving: 'Miles is not displeased. He is pleased. He has done his part. He has kept the faith. He turns off the lights. He locks the door.' The tug of the spiritual, the demands of marriage, the temptations of the material world and the preoccupation of the unique self, all pulling in different directions, is a familiar Updikean tension. Updike spent his life grappling intelligently with questions about faith and the afterlife. His position was simply that there can't be total extinction.

Updike was a diligent writer. He liked to get up after the domestic work was done, and he would work with intense concentration virtually every single day. I asked him what he thought about journalism, and he said he liked to see his name in print. His collections of his other work, starting with *Hugging the Shore* (1983), run routinely to 900 pages. One of his sons wrote that he applied a certain steeliness and single-mindedness to his writing, seldom compromising for the sake of the family. Updike loved women. Not long before he died he wrote a very warm memoir of his first wife, which seemed to me to be a sort of apology for his earlier behaviour. In my experience, serial adulterers, if they are also writers, feel faintly queasy as they grow older, both because of what they have done and what they have appropriated for their own ends.

My contact with Updike led to my being asked by him to write the foreword for a reissue of *Rabbit at Rest* (1990). I was, and still am, very proud to have my name in his book. His only comment was to say that his father was not a schoolmaster – as I had described him – but a teacher. He seemed to think that a schoolmaster was an administrator. I did not dare correct him.

Rabbit at Rest, I think, is the finest novel to come out of the last quarter of twentieth-century America. You will find lots of people who would disagree. There is something about his (mostly) realistic style, his gentlemanly demeanour, his attention to minor issues, as understood by his characters, and his lifelong project to depict his country in all its wisdom and foolishness, in its essential innocence and its longings, which has led some critics to underestimate him as rather mundane. It is true that his work was often about the quotidian, but it was written with wonderful deftness and originality. I think it was this perceived lack of interest in big issues that prevented him from being awarded the Nobel Prize. How many people really believe that Nadine Gordimer or Vargas Llosa or Doris Lessing are better writers than Updike?

The most difficult task for a writer is to make real and interesting an apparently unexceptional character. With *Rabbit at Rest*, Updike's dazzling achievement is to write about a man with little education, although Harry Angstrom now describes himself as a history buff; he is delving into his country's past in his retirement. Life, as Janice his long-suffering wife observes, has more or less been downhill all the way since he was a basketball star in high school. But Harry, who is weak, greedy and disloyal, is somehow true to a vision of himself and of a turbulent America. It is startlingly plausible. New York and New England don't impinge on Harry 'Rabbit' Angstrom's life or consciousness at all.

Rabbit is a man of Pennsylvania, and in a wider way an American archetype. Updike told me that he had never intended to write an extensive series of novels about Angstrom, each one separated by ten years almost by chance, but he had started the first novel because he was finding (if I remember correctly) a proposed book on the inept fifteenth president, James Buchanan, 'heavy going'. *Rabbit, Run* was published in 1960. In the subsequent novels Updike seized the opportunity to produce a sort of saga of the Angstrom family, led by Rabbit. By the arrival of *Rabbit at Rest*, Rabbit has grown fat and his health is not good. Here Updike's writing reaches extraordinary heights. Of course Rabbit still sees himself as tall and athletic, despite his appalling diet, which includes, inadvertently, some birdseed. Updike's sympathy for his character seems to me to have grown over the years.

His greatest skill to my mind was his ability to create characters out of the unremarked American middle class – a term which has a wholly different resonance from our own middle class – characters who live, even sing, out of their very ordinariness. Updike wrote that Rabbit is like the Underground Man, incorrigible; 'from first to last he bridles at good advice, taking direction only from his personal, also incorrigible, God'. What I see here is that behind the apparently effortless creation of the common man, Updike has in mind a universal character, and I don't think that it is at all fanciful to say that he was in his own way the American Dostoevsky, although I think he would have preferred to be compared to Nathaniel Hawthorne.

JUSTIN CARTWRIGHT has won many awards for his writing but doubts he'll ever be as famous as John Updike. His latest novel, *Up Against the Night*, has just been published.

A Light to Live by

SARAH PERRY

Late one summer afternoon, when I was perhaps 9 or 10, I found myself kneeling in the long grass of an Essex village common. It was towards the end of one of the chapel camping holidays we had each year, and with me were a dozen other children and those looking after us. I don't recall the name of the village, only that we'd walked a long way, and fetched up there in the last of the day's sun to remember the Colchester martyrs.

Hardly anyone thinks of them now, so that I find it hard to convey how significant a part of my youth was devoted to the commemoration of the 284 women and men burned alive during the reign of Mary Tudor. Essex saw so many pyres that it's studded all over with modest granite memorials or blue plaques fixed to what are now cafés or shoe-shops, and I could often be found standing in my father's shadow as he preached in their memory to Saturday shoppers passing by.

There on the village green someone handed me a leaflet and asked me to read aloud. On the cover was a drawing of a slender wrist held by a gloved hand; beneath the wrist was a candle held close. I began to read a story familiar to me: the account given in *Foxe's Book of Martyrs* of the torture of the Protestant Rose Allen. I remember how bright and still it was, and how relieved I felt that no one passing by wondered what we were doing, and drew near enough to hear the child reading how the young Rose, bringing a jug of water to her

Foxe's Book of Martyrs: Select Narratives
OUP · Pb · 384pp · £7.99 · ISBN 9780199236848

mother, was found by an interrogator in her own home; how he took her candle and moved it back and forth across her hand in the form of a cross until the tendons audibly cracked; and how later she thanked God she'd kept her temper, and not brought the jug down on her tormentor's head.

John Foxe was born in 1516, and after a studious youth took up a post as 'Lecturer of Logic' at Brasenose College, Oxford. He resigned on becoming a Protestant, pursuing his faith and conscience by writing in opposition to the death penalty for adultery, and on other contentious matters. On Mary Tudor's accession to the throne, feeling his life under threat, he went into exile in Europe; by the time he returned to England many of his friends and companions had been burned at the stake.

His *Book of Martyrs* stands alongside the King James Bible and the works of Shakespeare as among the most influential texts in the English language. Yet it also stands apart from any other, as being both a book and not a book; not quite history and not quite mere polemic. Even the title by which we know it is not its given name, and though it profoundly affected the development of the English consciousness, few – even among ardent bibliophiles – are familiar with its history.

On its publication by John Day in 1563 it was the largest and most complex book yet to be produced in English. It was a single volume too large to be held in one hand, and contained 60 woodcut illustrations of appalling accuracy. Its title was long and sonorous after the fashion of the time: 'The Actes and Monuments of these Latter and Perilous Days, Touching Matters of the Church' it begins, and continues for several clauses more. Dedicated to 'Elizabeth I, Our Gracious Lady Now Reygning', its purpose was to delineate the history of Christian martyrdom 'from the yeare of our Lorde a thousand unto the tyme now present'.

Church and public alike received the book with enthusiasm. Its ten-shilling price was roughly that of a month's wages to an ordinary man, but nonetheless it sold; and the Church ordered that it should be chained beside the bible in cathedrals, and that Church officials should keep a copy at home for the betterment of servants.

The source of its appeal is not difficult to discern. As a work of narrative it's like nothing so much as the *Canterbury Tales*: Bishop Bonner, who carried out Mary Tudor's orders with psychotic enthusiasm, is a villain to rival any found in literature, and its heroes – drawn largely from the labouring classes – are witty, brave, loving and flawed. There are moments of high drama and intense pathos, as friend is forced to turn on friend, or as illiterate spinners cheek their betters with memorized verses of scripture.

The ghoulish appetite for horror narrative, and for all the diligent details of the torturer's art, was never better satisfied than here. Foxe was unflinching in his recital of sufferings; in one account we learn how John Hooper 'knocked his breast with his hands, until one of his arms fell off, then knocked still with the other, what time the fat, water, and blood dropped out at his fingers' ends . . .'

For all its ghastly details the book was embraced as a devotional tool, inspiring a newly minted generation of Protestants to live more devoutly. The final words of the martyrs, often mingled with pleas for better wood to be brought to hasten the end, would have been especially moving: 'Lord Jesus, receive my spirit.' That Foxe's account includes those martyrs whose faith wavered as they saw sparks struck in the distance only intensifies their appeal. The moment Thomas Cranmer holds to the flames the hand that signed a recantation of his faith, so that the treacherous limb would burn before any other part of his body, rivals any scene in Shakespeare.

The book was also an important political tool, and one enthusiastically employed by the Virgin Queen and her court. Here, in black and white, were the consequences of a Papist regime, from which all England had so narrowly escaped! If ever a book were to turn the citizenry in gratitude to its ruler, it was this.

In response to its immediate popularity, Foxe produced a second and greatly expanded edition seven years later. The 1570 version ran to two volumes, and 2,300 folio pages. The politicization of the book may be traced in the gradual changing of its title: there was no mention of England in the first edition, but by the second readers were plainly informed they were to read of 'thynges passed . . . specially in the Church of England'. By the third edition the intent to foment a loathing of the Catholic Church was still more plain, as the title refers explicitly to 'tumults styred up by Romish prelates in the Church'. Foxe was exasperated by the public's insistence on referring to his 'Book of Martyrs', whatever title he himself imposed. 'I wrote no such booke bearying the title Booke of Martyrs,' he wrote, but he was roundly ignored. The edition I have before me – a white paperback published by Oxford University Press, featuring exclusively the Marian martyrs – is of course entitled *Foxe's Book of Martyrs: Select Narratives*.

The reliability of the book as historical record is troublesome in the extreme, and a question unsettled despite centuries of academic consideration. Foxe was thorough in his use of sources, from Josephus and Bede to court transcripts, eyewitness testimony and letters in contemporary accounts. When challenged as to the truthfulness of his reports, he was not above removing whole portions of text from subsequent editions; at other times, convinced of his accuracy, he'd produce avalanches of supporting evidence with which to bury his accuser.

Yet for all his evident attempts at compiling a historically accurate record, Foxe made not the least pretence at objectivity. He's a decidedly present narrator, and his bitter loathing of the Catholic Church and his firm belief in what he considered Protestant truth is evident throughout. No wonder then that to English Catholics living under the restraints brought in by Elizabeth I – unable to hold public office, denied religious freedom, suffering punitive taxes – Foxe's book was an act of devastating untruth. It was 'a stinking dunghill' of 'a thousand lies', despaired the priest Thomas Harding. Late into the eighteenth century it was credited with stirring anti-Catholic sentiment: the Catholic bishop John Milner in 1795 called it 'that lying book'. It almost certainly played a role in developing that part of the English consciousness which even now seems to be permanently expecting the Spanish Inquisition: the suspicion that beyond the borders, on Europe's rather more Papal shores, there wait ranks of purple-robed priests bent on persecuting the simple-hearted English peasantry. I've no way of knowing if UKIP's headquarters conceals a copy of Foxe, but I would not be altogether surprised.

Looking now at those iconic woodcuts – Rose Allen holding her jug of water; Cranmer putting his hand to the flame – it's possible to conceive of Foxe's work as having passed away in a merciful age of religious tolerance: a remarkable curiosity, but little more. But I remain in thrall to its stories, perhaps because – almost uniquely among the great works of British history – it dwells on the lives of the women and the common men. As a child, leafing with delicious horror through my father's eighteenth-century edition, so big it barely fitted on my lap, I did not understand that I was reading not only about acts of profound religious faith, but of political radicalism. To defy the Church was to defy the State, and Foxe's work provides a remarkable account of housewives and spinsters, illiterate boys and elderly men prepared to die rather than have their consciences dictated to by palace or parliament.

When I think of Rose Allen now, she seems to me to stand beside Malala Yousafzai: an ordinary girl possessed of extraordinary courage in defiance of those who'd take away her right to freedom of thought, or to study in her own language. When I read of the poor illiterate woman known only as Prest's wife, turned out of her home by her sons for failing to attend Mass and then burned for her scruples, I think of courageous women the world over moving quietly against repressive regimes. When the editor of a Paris satirical magazine was murdered with his staff, the fact that he was reported to have said 'I'd rather die on my feet than live on my knees' made me think of the

19-year-old weaver's apprentice from Brentwood, who died rather than give up the right to read the Bible in his own language, and work out his own faith.

Foxe recounts the deaths of Hugh Latimer and Nicholas Ridley, burned together in a ditch near Balliol College, Oxford. Wanting to give his friend courage as the wood was stacked around them, Latimer said: 'Be of good comfort Master Ridley . . . we shall this day light such a candle by God's grace in England, as I trust shall never be put out.' I hope it's not too fanciful to think that the candle never did go out, not quite: perhaps it's not wholly the flame they'd imagined, and perhaps it has at times burned low; but so long as we enjoy freedom of conscience, there's enough light to live by.

SARAH PERRY was born in Essex. Brought up in a devoutly religious home, she was kept largely apart from contemporary culture and spent her youth immersed in the King James Bible and in Christian history and literature. Her first novel, *After Me Comes the Flood*, was published in 2014.

Joining the Grown-ups

MATTHEW ADAMS

When I was about 9 or 10, my great passions in life were dogs, football, books, my grandparents' farm, and a young man who lived in the house next door. I found him impossibly glamorous. He was seven years my senior, he went to pubs, he wore a leather jacket, he had daringly short black hair and sported an earring, he smoked, and he radiated a carelessness and confidence that I hoped might rub off on me – an awkward, shy, slight boy, ridiculously grave and perpetually worried, whose only notable similarity to his neighbour was that he shared his name: he was known as 'Big Matt', I was 'Little Matt'. Still, he *noticed* me. He would talk to me about school and offer me spectacularly inappropriate advice about girls. He would play me records and make me compilation tapes. He would take me to play football and furnish me with the shirts of his favourite (and hence my favourite) club. Big Matt, it was said, could do no wrong. Until, one day, Big Matt broke Little Matt's heart.

I can still see the expression, the lined concern, on my father's face as he prepared to tell me the news. 'No,' I said, and cut off his attempt to repeat himself with a desperate restatement of my position: 'NO!' There followed a bewildering sense of incomprehension. How could Big Matt be leaving? How could Big Matt be leaving for *another country?* How could Big Matt be leaving for another country to take up a post *in the army?* All colour drained from my world.

When Big Matt did eventually leave, three indecently short weeks after my father broke the news of his departure, I took refuge in the company of my dog: we would brood together, walk together, read together, we would daydream together about what Big Matt might be up to. After a while I started to inflict my curiosity on my father. 'Dad? What do you think Big Matt's doing?' 'Dad? What's it like being in the army?' 'Dad? What are wars like?' In time my questions got a bit more sophisticated: 'Dad? Why do we *have* an army?' 'Dad? How *long* have we had an army?' 'Dad? How many wars has Britain fought?' 'Dad? Are armies what *make history?*' My father coped with my questions patiently, but I am sure he had at least one eye on his sanity when one day after work he said: 'There's a book on the table you might be interested in . . .'

I didn't pick it up straight away but eventually I did settle down with it: *Escape from France*, by Ronald Welch . . .

I read it in two enraptured sittings. I loved Richard Carey, the hero of the novel: his charm and glamour reminded me of Big Matt, but he was thrilling on his own terms, too. And the action of the book, which takes place in the midst of the French Revolution, was equally seductive and electrifying. Bless my dad: I didn't need to ask for the other books in the series. He would notice I had finished one and return with volume after volume, leaving each on the kitchen table with barely a word. Before long I had acquainted myself with the entire history of the members of the Carey family, from their activities in *Knight Crusader*, set during the Third Crusade, all the way up to *Nicholas Carey*, which ends in the Crimean War.

Revisiting the Carey novels today, I am struck by how fresh and magnetizing they have remained, and by how much there is in these books – as there is in all good children's literature – that can be enjoyed by adults. It is common for readers of Welch to credit him with sparking a love of history (I know an Oxford scholar of medieval literature who says she owes her career to Welch); what we hear less often is how subtle and careful his use of history can be. *Escape from France* and *Nicholas Carey* work brilliantly as historical fiction because the history with which they are suffused is always given a human face.

History, here, is about people, and in focusing on people, these books remind us just how haphazard the evolution of the past can be:

William Stobbs

how events are determined not just by policies and 'the subtly laid schemes of statesmen', as another great historical novelist, George MacDonald Fraser, has his Flashman tell us, but 'by someone's having a bellyache, or not sleeping well, or a sailor getting drunk, or some aristocratic harlot waggling her backside'.

In both *Escape from France* and *Nicholas Carey*, much of the action is driven not by events but by accidents of character, reputation, social and familial connection: it is the 'unwritten rule, that a Carey helped a Carey', that comes to the rescue of the Emperor of France in *Nicholas Carey*, just as in *Escape from France* the safety of Quentin d'Assailly (head of the French side of the Carey family) depends not on Richard's conscious application, but on his natural resilience and stoicism, and his unwitting brilliance as a swordsman.

When Welch does introduce the reader to major historical events or major historical figures, he tends to do so from the perspective of the street, so that both his heroes and his readers encounter them with the same kind of fleeting immediacy that an ordinary person of the period might have done. Here is Richard Carey, in the heart of Paris in the middle of the French Revolution:

Then he heard a different sound, the clip-clop of many hooves, and a squadron of cavalry trotted past; the crowds swayed and pushed, and fell silent. Richard craned his head out of the window. But there was little to see, except the dense masses of horsemen, and in the centre a large green coach that rumbled swiftly over the cobbles. Richard caught a brief glimpse of a brown-coated man inside, a calm, white face and a high forehead, and King Louis had passed.

William Stobbs

This is just one instance of Welch's remarkable understanding of restraint. How magical to find ourselves on the streets of Paris, afforded only a glimpse of the passing Louis; how tawdry a more prolonged encounter would be.

I remember feeling the frisson of this brush with history when I first read the book. Yet what appealed to me most at the time, and part of what I find most admirable now, is the human sensibility of these stories: what they have to say about what it is to be somebody who feels ill-equipped for the world, who feels he or she has no natural place, who feels forever on the brink of being found out – a perpetual Little Matt. Both Richard and Nicholas Carey are troubled by these emotions; Nicholas suffers particularly acutely. In the novel that bears his name, which begins in Italy in 1853 and concludes in the Crimea in 1855, Nicholas is presented as an officer in the army who has never seen combat; an artist with 'a liking for solitude' who has never exerted himself at anything. He feels lazy, and without a vestige of ambition. His childhood, we learn, had been a somewhat lonely one.

Yet as the novel progresses, we begin to see these feelings of insecurity and ineptitude subside. Thrust into a world of action, Nicholas begins to grow up. Not because he has decided to, but because the world has awakened in him qualities that were always there, and he finds himself filled with the exhilaration of a man who suddenly discovers he can lead.

This is the message that recurs throughout these wonderful novels: that we are invariably better equipped than we believe ourselves to be. There may always be a part of us that feels, as Richard Carey does, 'a mere child, a beginner, a sheer amateur', assailed by the sense that we are in 'the middle of a dream where you try to run, and your arms and legs refuse to move'. Yet in tandem with this truth, Welch reminds us that we are also, all of us, potentially remarkable beings, all deserving of admiration and affection, all capable of that which we fear is beyond us – all capable, in fact, of noticing the talents of ourselves and others, of venturing forth into the world, and becoming our own Big Matts.

MATTHEW ADAMS writes and reviews for a number of publications, including the *Spectator*, the *Literary Review*, the *Independent* and the *Guardian*. He still feels he is on the verge of being found out – but he doesn't let that stop him. He is working on a novel.

Ronald Welch's *Escape from France* (192pp) and *Nicholas Carey* (224pp) are both available from *Slightly Foxed* in a new limited and numbered clothbound edition of 2,000 copies, each priced at £16 (UK), £18 (Europe) or £19 (Rest of World). All prices include post and packing. Copies may be ordered by post (53 Hoxton Square, London N1 6PB), by phone (020 7033 0258) or via our website www.foxedquarterly.com.

ALSO AVAILABLE NOW
Knight Crusader, Bowman of Crécy,
The Galleon, The Hawk, For the King,
Captain of Dragoons and *Captain of Foot*

FORTHCOMING
March 2016 *Mohawk Valley*
September 2016 *Ensign Carey* and *Tank Commander*

If you would like to order a set of all 12 titles with the same limited-edition number, please call the office on 020 7033 0258 or email us at all@foxedquarterly.com.

From Chicago to the Western Front

BEL MOONEY

One day I was sorting out the collection of thrillers in the spare room when I glanced up at the watercolour of a beautiful woman that has hung on a wall there for four years, since we moved house. She is in profile, wearing the crisply billowing headdress of a nurse, her lowered gaze calm and reflective. The portrait used to hang in the guest room of my former house and before that in the hall of the farm I shared with my first husband. At some point in the Seventies he and I had bought it from the long-established London dealers Abbott & Holder, but it came with no information – except the name and date in the top right-hand corner, 'Mary Spears 1918', and the faint monogram CGD in the lower left.

Something made me take it from the wall. Her face had always captivated me, so why was she relegated to a room I rarely visit? And why had I never bothered to find out who she was? Out of sight, out of mind . . . But nowadays it is easy; a quick Internet search revealed that this saintly-looking nurse was in fact an acclaimed and popular novelist, and the author of a powerful First World War memoir.

Mary Spears was born Mary (or May) Borden in 1886, the beautiful, capricious and intelligent daughter of a Chicago millionaire. At 20 she came into her fortune and escaped her stifling family to travel

Mary Borden, *The Forbidden Zone* (1929) · Hesperus · Pb · 152pp · £7.99 · ISBN 9781843914433; Jane Conway, *Mary Borden: A Woman of Two Wars* (2009) · Munday · Pb · 260pp · £9.99 · ISBN 9780956329707. Mary Borden's poems appear in Tim Kendall (ed.), *Poetry of the First World War: An Anthology* (2013) · OUP · Hb · 368pp · £14.99 · ISBN 9780199581443.

the world in search of excitement. Unfortunately she also made an unwise marriage to a missionary called Douglas Turner, but by the outbreak of the First World War she had become a celebrated literary hostess in London, establishing herself as a writer and mixing with the great men of the day, including George Bernard Shaw, E. M. Forster, Ford Madox Ford and Ezra Pound. A keen suffragist and independent spirit, she became Wyndham Lewis's lover and bought his work. Then, in 1916, she met her great love, the handsome, brave and charismatic Edward Louis Spears, an Anglo-Irish lieutenant in the French army. Her divorce from Turner and the custody battle over their children was bloody, but Mary and Edward married in 1918. Perhaps Edward commissioned the distinguished artist Charles

Geoffroy-Dechaume (yes, I identified the monogram too) to draw Mary in the uniform she was wearing when he met her – to mark their wedding.

Mary Borden's experiences during both world wars make extraordinary reading. I recommend Jane Conway's fine biography, *A Woman of Two Wars*, for the full story of a vivid, original and courageous woman who deserves to be better known. The First World War plunged this privileged, head-strong young Anglo-American into a maelstrom of horror that she was to record in her memoir *The Forbidden Zone* (1929). Her account in it of nursing on the Western Front is enthralling, heartbreaking, haunting. Fragments of prose splinter from the page; weariness and despair are transformed through art. I do not understand why she is not ranked as one of the finest chroniclers of the Great War, and one of the few considerable female poets. But it is time to rediscover the talent of Lady Spears, as she became.

In 1915, when she had only recently given birth to her third child, Mary set off for France. She had no nursing experience and no French, but she did have money and determination. She set up her own field hospital and there, confronting the horrors of war night and day, somehow she still found time to raise funds from America and to write. Her hospital had the lowest mortality rate on the Western Front, and her humanitarian work later won her not only the Croix de Guerre but also the Légion d'honneur.

Borden begins *The Forbidden Zone* with a surprisingly bald statement: 'I have not invented anything in this book.' She explains that the sketches and poems were written between 1914 and 1918 but the stories are more recent and recount 'true episodes I cannot forget'. The paradox becomes clear: she is telling the truth and yet the truth was so dreadful that 'I have blurred the bare horror of facts and softened the reality in spite of myself . . .'

She divides the book into three parts: The North, The Somme and Poems. The opening sentences of the first chapter, 'Belgium', plunge the reader, as if *in medias res*, into the wasteland:

Mud: and a thin rain coming down to make more mud.

Mud: with scraps of iron lying in it and the straggling fragment of a nation, lolling, hanging about in the mud, on the edge of disaster.

It is quiet here. The rain and the mud muffle the voice of the war that is growling beyond the horizon. But if you listen you can hear cataracts of iron pouring down channels in the sodden land, and you feel the earth trembling.

The poetic prose is personal, immediate, grabbing you with a skinny hand like the Ancient Mariner and insisting that you open your eyes and look:

This is what is left of Belgium. Come, I'll show you. Here are trees drooping along a canal, ploughed fields, roads leading into sand dunes, roofless houses. There's a farm, an old woman with a crooked back feeding chickens, a convoy of motor lorries round a barn; they squat like elephants. And here is a village crouching in the mud: the cobblestone street is slippery and smeared with refuse and there is a yellow cat sitting in a window. This is the headquarters of the Belgian Army. You see those men, lolling in the doorways – uncouth, dishevelled, dirty? They are soldiers. You can read on their heavy jowls, in their stupefied, patient, hopeless eyes, how boring it is to be a hero.

This is not so much the pity of war as the dreary, endless ugliness of war. Not even the officers with their privileges will escape: 'They wear fine uniforms. Their faces are clean. They have been eating good food . . . They wear gloves. They will be destroyed with their gold braid and their medals and the good food inside them.' This staccato style expresses the mood of harsh acceptance that permeates *The Forbidden Zone*; not acceptance of man's inhumanity to man, but of the implacable fate that will play with human beings, pitilessly.

The writer who had delighted in witty, well-informed conversation in salons now listens to 'the boy's . . . choking and shuddering . . . and every few seconds . . . a wail of defiant terror'. The fashionable woman who dressed for dinner now sees herself ironically through the wrong end of a telescope: 'You fuss about busily. You move your feet and rustle your petticoats . . . You have stained your fingers. There is a spot on your white apron; but you are superb . . .' The confident socialite who had travelled the world now finds herself demolished by the emotional need of a blinded soldier who thinks his nurse has left him alone: 'Sister! My sister! Where are you?' To the dismay of her veteran male orderlies this encounter briefly breaks Mary's spirit: 'At that I fled from him. I ran down the long, dreadful hut and hid behind my screen and cowered, sobbing, in a corner, hiding my face.'

What makes *The Forbidden Zone* such a unique testament is its very modern approach to style. It is neither reportage, nor memoir, nor fiction, but a combination of all three. No two chapters are alike: 'Paraphernalia' is a dry exercise in bitter self-mockery, 'In the Operating Room' is written like a Radio 4 play, and 'The Priest and the Rabbi' reads like a fable. 'Rosa' is the gripping account of a nurse's moral dilemma, faced with a would-be suicide who could be saved, but who would then be shot for desertion. 'Blind' has such an intensity that reportage is lifted to the economical exactitude of the novella. You read without knowing how she will shift her style to encompass the variety of experience, or if she will falter and beg you to share her trauma: 'Looking back, I do not understand that woman – myself – standing in that confused goods yard filled with bundles of broken human flesh. The place by one o'clock in the morning was a shambles. The air was thick with steaming sweat, with the effluvia of mud, dirt, blood.'

Her anger and frustration are beautifully contained: 'There has been a harvest. Crops of men were cut down in the fields of France where they were growing. They were mown down with a scythe, were gathered into bundles, tossed about with pitchforks . . . scattered by storms and gathered up again and at last brought here – what was left of them.' The writer-turned-nurse uses bold metaphor to make us see the wounded men anew: 'Pain is the mistress of them . . . you can watch her plying her trade here any day. She is shameless. She lies in their beds all day . . . she never leaves them . . . she lies there to spoil their dreams.'

With no sentimentality, Mary beckons you to view the suffering with such pity that, like her, you recognize death as a welcome grace: 'There's not a sound except the whisper of the wind in the grass. Quick! Be quick! In a moment a man's spirit will escape, will be flying through the night past the pale, beautiful sentimental face of the moon.'

And then there are the poems which form the last part of *The Forbidden Zone*. They have the loping, declamatory power of Walt Whitman but they do not sing majestically like his poems. Instead they almost wail, in broken disbelief. 'Where Is Jehovah' and 'The Virgin of Albert' spit on the altars of a Christian faith which could do nothing to avert the horror of war, while the best poem, 'Unidentified', is a litany of mourning for the doomed unknown soldier who, at the point of death, remembers 'what he loved and what he wanted, and what he never had'.

This woman was extraordinary. In the Second World War she set up another field hospital in France and, as the Germans advanced, barely escaped with her life. Later she founded a mobile unit for the Free French in Palestine. Yet she remains little known. *The Forbidden Zone* was published in the same year as *A Farewell to Arms, Goodbye to All That* and *All Quiet on the Western Front* – and maybe that was the trouble. Critical reception was mixed, and some people found Mary's book too graphic. Personally I don't think they could stomach the fact that this angry, beautiful, true book was written by a woman – and one who was *there*.

BEL MOONEY has written six novels, nearly thirty children's books, a memoir called *A Small Dog Saved My Life* and millions of words of journalism. She is currently translating an Anglo-Saxon elegy into modern English for fun, and wishes she were a student once more.

Modern Life Is Rubbish

HENRY JEFFERYS

It was eerie the first time I watched *The Fall and Rise of Reginald Perrin* because it all felt so familiar. I'd bought a DVD box-set on a whim. Suddenly my parents' baffling banter made sense. When I thought they were speaking gibberish they were in fact quoting Perrin. My mother would say 'great' and my father would say 'super'. My father would say things like 'I didn't get where I am today' and my mother would say 'I'm not a committee person.' If lunch was going to be late my father would say 'bit of a cock-up on the catering front'. They'd been doing it so long that I doubt they even knew they were speaking Perrinese. It's difficult to overstate how thoroughly Perrin has seeped into popular culture and language.

The TV series starring Leonard Rossiter was based on a novel, *The Death of Reginald Perrin* by David Nobbs, published in 1975. Its eponymous hero is Reginald Iolanthe Perrin (Iolanthe because his mother was meant to appear in the Gilbert and Sullivan operetta but had to bow out when she became pregnant). You'll note the initials, RIP. Reggie's inane job as middle manager at a convenience pudding company, Sunshine Desserts, is sending him slowly mad. He lives on a neo-Georgian estate where all the roads are named after famous poets in the (fictional) South London suburb of Climthorpe. He's married to Elizabeth and has two children – Mark, a failed or rather

David Nobbs, *The Death of Reginald Perrin* (1975), *The Return of Reginald Perrin* (1977) and *The Better World of Reginald Perrin* (1978) are available in a single volume, *The Reginald Perrin Omnibus* (Arrow · Pb · 896pp · £16.99 · ISBN 9780099436669).

failing actor, and Linda who is married to Tom, an estate agent whom Reggie dislikes. Linda and Tom have two children, Adam and Jocasta. Reggie catches the same train with the same people every day. At work his boss is the overbearing CJ who says things like 'I didn't get where I am today without recognizing a favourable report when I see one.' His colleagues are Tony and David who say 'great' and 'super' respectively after everything anyone senior says, and he fantasizes about seducing his secretary Joan.

CJ thinks that Reggie is losing his 'drive' and indeed Reggie is temporarily impotent. Worse still, Reggie has anarchic urges that he finds impossible to control. This is the opening line of the book: 'When Reginald Iolanthe Perrin set out for work on the Thursday morning, he had no intention of calling his mother-in-law a hippopotamus. Nothing could have been further from his thoughts.'

Random words such as 'parsnips' pop out of his mouth at unexpected moments, and as the novel progresses his behaviour becomes increasingly erratic: he invites CJ and other colleagues to a dinner party but doesn't serve any food; he gets out of his car amidst a pride of lions at a wildlife park; and he gets drunk at a conference where he's meant to be giving the keynote speech. It's not spoiling the plot too much to say that he then disappears, having faked his own suicide, and adopts a series of increasingly outlandish assumed personas.

The first series follows the plot of the book extremely closely but in some ways they are very different. The television programme is held together by the madcap energy of Rossiter who positively twitches with frustrated passions. He looks like a man trying very hard, but failing, to be normal. The Reggie of the book is more of an Everyman and so his outbursts and erratic behaviour surprise us. He reminds me of the baffled Englishman with a pipe from the Matt cartoons in the *Daily Telegraph*. He's Pooter from *The Diary of a Nobody* who has just realized that his life is pointless.

Nothing works properly in Reggie's Britain: trains are always late, his car breaks down in the wildlife park, even his zip gets stuck. It's a very '70s kind of malaise. A running theme in the book is how bad the 'tasteless chemical beer' has become. It's the era of Watney's Red Barrel, and the big brewers are trying to phase out traditional beer. The pubs are being knocked through and now serve 'eggs styled to your choice'. The old ways are dying out and being replaced with modern imitations.

It's telling that Reggie works for a company that makes ersatz puddings. Beyond the period references, however, there's something timeless about his dissatisfaction: David Nobbs taps into a peculiarly English kind of melancholy. When drunk, 'Reggie expressed his regret for the passing of the steam engine, the brass bedstead and the pyjama cord.' It's that nostalgia for a lost England that one finds in *Village Green Preservation Society* by the Kinks or more recently Blur's *Modern Life Is Rubbish*. In fact that could be an alternative title.

The book has an elegiac quality that plays second fiddle in the series to the comedy. A good comparison would be *Coming up for Air*. Like George Bowling in George Orwell's novel, Perrin is fighting fruitlessly against modernity. Orwell writes: 'There's a chap who thinks he's going to escape! There's a chap who says he won't be streamlined! He's going back to Lower Binfield! After him! Stop him!' The Perrin equivalent is: 'People are graded too . . . They're sorted out. The right ones are packed off to management training schemes. They're standardized . . .' In fact there's a moment towards the end of the novel which is straight out of *Coming up for Air*. Reggie goes back to the village where he used to holiday and runs into his boyhood crush. She has grown old and coarse, and doesn't recognize him. 'It had all been a terrible mistake,' Reggie says.

The tone of the book is darker than the television series. In the book Elizabeth's brother Jimmy has an affair with his niece Linda, whereas in the series they only flirt. We're explicitly told that the reason Jimmy keeps popping over so amusingly to borrow food – 'bit of a cock-up on the catering front' – is because his wife is an alcoholic and she's spent every penny on drink. There's even a hint of suburban anti-Semitism: Reggie's neighbours, the Wisemans, are informed that there are no vacancies at the golf club. Towards the end, we learn that Joan's husband, who keeps nearly being cuckolded by Reggie, is in a vegetative state in a hospital following, we assume, an accident. After another failed attempt to have sex with Joan, Reggie is described as 'shaking with humiliation and anger and frustration'.

The darkness doesn't detract from the humour, however. The book is built on a number of comic set pieces to rival P. G. Wodehouse or Evelyn Waugh: Reggie's drunken speech to the British Fruit Society, his flight across England in a lorry shaped like a fruit flan and, funniest of all, his attendance at his own wake disguised as one Martin Wellborn. In fact the book is packed with some of the most memorable characters in English literature: there's CJ of course; Elizabeth's brother Jimmy, a buttoned-up ex-Army man who can't get the hang of Civvy Street; Doc Morrissey, the incompetent doctor at Sunshine Desserts; and Tom, Reggie's politically correct son-in-law. There are surreal one-liners too. A newspaper headline declares: 'Council house armadillo ban protest march row'. Jimmy tells a story about a soldier who went insane and thought he was a deckchair: 'No can do. I'm a deckchair.' And after his 'suicide' Reggie ponders changing his name to Colin: 'He felt an incipient colinishness.'

It's the men who get the best lines, and in its treatment of the female characters the book does betray its age. It's a very different England where executives are almost expected to try to seduce their secretaries. Reggie is losing his drive, but what about his poor long-suffering wife Elizabeth? Sunshine Desserts may be a nightmare for Reggie but with its company doctor, canteen and long holidays it would look like a model employer nowadays.

Yet in other ways Nobbs's book is uncannily up-to-date. Reggie is baffled by his son's cockney accent. Tom and Linda are practising non-disciplinarian parenting, so their children are allowed to run riot. We also derive much humour from Tom's pious interest in organic food and home-brewing. The preoccupation with Europe could be my father at Sunday lunch: 'By 1977 the whole of Europe will have achieved standardization of draught beer, pork pies and envelope sizes.' Reggie is baffled into silence at work by meaningless jargon and spurious statistics.

The book has a wisdom about it that makes repeated readings worthwhile. Doc Morrissey says to Reggie: 'Characters in books are always over-sexed. Authors hope it'll be taken as autobiographical.' At one point Reggie thinks, 'Our children remind us of our enormous capacity for folly.' Yet despite all the sadness and darkness, the book ends on a warm note as Reggie realizes how much he loves and misses Elizabeth. The finale sees him back in the bosom of his family. He's even happy to see Tom, who has almost the last word: 'That's what life's all about. People. We're people people.'

The television series appeared a year after the book was first published. It was an instant hit, so naturally the BBC wanted to make another series. Leonard Rossiter, however, insisted David Nobbs write two more novels and then adapt them for television. The second series is wonderful, perhaps as good as the first, but the third is patchy. The BBC went on scraping the barrel after Rossiter's death with a fourth series in which Geoffrey Palmer played Jimmy as the lead. The absolute nadir, however, was the recent remake starring Martin Clunes, about which the less said the better.

Ignore the television series if you can because the first Reggie Perrin novel deserves to be considered a classic in its own right. It's not only extremely funny but it provides a guide to moving gracefully into middle age. The age I am now, much closer to 40 than 30, is perhaps the best time to read it. In fact I think I feel an incipient Reggieness coming on. Parsnips.

HENRY JEFFERYS is a wine columnist. He is currently writing *Empire of Booze,* a history of Britain told through alcoholic drinks.

The Green Notebook

AMY LIPTROT

It might be irresponsible to recommend Louise Fitzhugh's *Harriet the Spy* (1964) to youngsters today, with its sulky, unrepentant heroine who snoops on neighbours and whose notebook entries result in her losing friends. They might like it as much as I did. My copy, kept safe through house sales and moves and decades, is the only childhood book I still have, my best and most important. I've written inside the front cover: 'Amy M. Liptrot, Private Spy. This book is totally brilliant!'

Growing up on a farm on the Scottish island of Orkney, I had no idea what a luncheonette and egg cream were, or cocktails and a dumb waiter, but rereading the mysterious words now brings a rush of affection for their familiar patterns. At the age of 8 or 9, back in the late '80s, it was simply a book about a cool, brave American girl who spies on her neighbours and who wants to be an author one day. Harriet writes (usually in block capitals): 'WHEN I GROW UP I'M GOING TO FIND OUT EVERYTHING ABOUT EVERYBODY AND PUT IT ALL IN A BOOK. THE BOOK IS GOING TO BE CALLED *SECRETS* BY HARRIET M. WELSCH. I WILL ALSO HAVE PHOTOGRAPHS IN IT AND MAYBE SOME MEDICAL CHARTS IF I CAN GET THEM.'

Living in a 1960s New York townhouse with both a cook and a nanny, 11-year-old Harriet is the only child of often absent parents. Her mother lunches and plays bridge (which Harriet thinks is boring) and her father 'works in television'. Each day, after school,

Louise Fitzhugh, *Harriet the Spy* (1964)
HarperCollins · Pb · 288pp · £9.99 · ISBN 9780007333868

Harriet takes a 'spy route' around her neighbourhood in Eastside Manhattan, writing in her green notebook about the people she watches through windows and skylights, from fire escapes and – audaciously – by climbing into a dumb waiter.

These risky adventures are accompanied by Fitzhugh's own illustrations of the people Harriet spies on: Agatha K. Plumber, a rich divorcée who lies in bed and talks on the phone all day; a grocery shop and the Italian family who run it; the Robinsons, a couple who 'think they're perfect' and buy a monstrous modern art statue of a baby; and Harrison Withers, who makes birdcages and has twenty-five cats with names like Rasputin, Puck and Cassandra. Fitzhugh's own prejudices and frustrations with society play out through the eyes of a child. Of Agatha K. Plumber, Harriet writes: 'HOW DOES SHE PAY FOR ANYTHING JUST LYING THERE? I GUESS SHE JUST LIVES OFF HER HUSBAND'S MONEY'; and of Harrison Withers, 'I WOULDN'T MIND LIVING LIKE HARRISON WITHERS BECAUSE HE ALWAYS LOOKS HAPPY.'

Harriet wears a belt hung with her 'spy tools' (a flashlight, a pouch for a notebook, a case for pens, a water canteen and a Boy Scout knife), eats only tomato sandwiches, uses American slang ('oh boy') and wears black-rimmed spectacles with no glass in them. At school she passes notes to members of her weird gang: serious Sport, who looks after his writer father (I now realize he's an alcoholic – '"Why do you eat so late?" "He has cocktails first."'), and Janie, an aspiring scientist. The details combine to create an attractive picture of a child writer, a tomboy in practical clothes who says things like, 'I'll be FINKED if I go to dancing school.'

Nanny 'Ole Golly' – terrific, strange, literature-loving, decisive – has been with Harriet since she was born, and is a stable counterpoint to her distracted parents. She tells Harriet, 'If you are ever going to be a writer it is time you got cracking. You are eleven years old . . .' There's a joyous sequence when Ole Golly and her fiancé take Harriet to the cinema. With the three of them on one bike,

Anna Trench

Harriet inside the delivery basket with Ole Golly sitting on top, 'they whirled down the hill and zoomed over into Eighty-Sixth Street'.

Harriet has been writing since she was 8, and is now on her fifteenth notebook. She is brave and inquisitive but she's also arrogant ('I will be a spy and know everything'), throws tantrums and is often cruel. The notebook contains candid observations of classmates – some show she is beginning to understand the world and how she fits in, some are just nasty. 'THE REASON SPORT DRESSES SO FUNNY IS THAT HIS FATHER WON'T BUY HIM ANYTHING TO WEAR BECAUSE HIS MOTHER HAS ALL THE MONEY'; 'MISS ELLISON HAS A WART BEHIND HER ELBOW.'

The mood of the book turns after the delivery-bike episode. Harriet's parents accuse Ole Golly of putting Harriet in danger and dismiss her, though in fact no one cares about Harriet as much as Ole Golly does. Then, during a game of catch, Harriet's notebook is read by classmates who, hurt and appalled, turn on Harriet and form a 'Spy Catcher Club', playing tricks on her and stealing her sandwiches. We know that Harriet doesn't dislike them and has just been honest in her notebook, but her frustration at being misunderstood and turned on by friends is painfully compelling and says much about the complex allegiances of schoolchildren.

When the diary is confiscated, Harriet is despondent: 'She found that when she didn't have a notebook, it was hard to think.' She is sent to a psychiatrist whom she charms with her precocity. 'I will never give up this notebook but it is clear that they are going to be as mean as they can until I do. They just don't know Harriet M. Welsch,' she writes. She is not only determined to be a writer, but also perhaps is unable to be anything else.

The ending is tough. Although Harriet's parents apologize, her much-loved Ole Golly does not return. Instead she writes Harriet a final letter. 'I never miss anyone or anything because it becomes a lovely memory,' she says, and then she gives some uncomfortable advice: 'Sometimes you have to lie. But to yourself you must always tell the truth.' Harriet is learning to balance honesty with her need for friendship, but despite her experiences, she refuses to change and continues her gossip and observations in the school newspaper. She wants to write about what she thinks really happens and what really matters, and in that she has chosen to take a difficult path.

It was with Harriet that I discovered the possibility of another, inner, life. Her secret notebook ('I never go anywhere without it') got me started on writing my own. My notebooks became diaries, which later became blogs and journalism. Now, writing in my notebook with a duvet tented over my back, I've reconnected with the little girl I was: the 9-year-old spy, who identified with an American girl with a green composition notebook and a profession.

AMY LIPTROT grew up on a sheep farm. Since returning to Orkney three years ago, she has spent summers working for the RSPB and winters living on the tiny island of Papa Westray where she has been writing her first book, *The Outrun*.

A Terrible Hidden Country

ANTHONY WELLS

If there were quiz questions about the subtitles of books, this – 'An Experiment in Literary Investigation' – might be among the trickier ones, offering as it does no hint of the book's subject matter. But a taster of what is to follow, and of the reason behind the subtitle, comes at once in the book's preface.

In 1949 – it begins – the author and some friends came across a noteworthy news item in the Soviet scientific magazine *Nature*. It reported that in the course of excavations on the Kolyma River in Siberia, prehistoric fauna tens of thousands of years old had been discovered in a frozen stream. These fish, or salamander, the report continued, were preserved in so fresh a state that, in the words of the *Nature* correspondent (but with the author's italics) 'those present immediately broke open the ice encasing the specimens and devoured them *with relish* on the spot'.

What was the significance of this incident? The readers of *Nature* might have struggled to understand why anyone would fall on precious prehistoric fish and gobble them up, but the author and his friends understood instantly:

> We understood because we ourselves were the same kind of people as those present at the event. We, too, were from that

The three volumes of *The Gulag Archipelago* (1973) in English are out of print, but an edition abridged into one volume at the author's wish and with his full co-operation is available: Alexander Solzhenitsyn, *The Gulag Archipelago* · Trans. Thomas P. Whitney & Harry Willets · Harvill · Pb · 496pp · £16.99 · ISBN 9781843430858.

powerful tribe of zeks, unique on the face of the earth, the only people who could devour prehistoric salamander *with relish*.

The author is our guide not just to the tribe of zeks but to their country, too:

> And the Kolyma was the greatest and most famous island, the pole of ferocity of that amazing country of *Gulag* which, though scattered in an Archipelago geographically, was, in the psycho-logical sense, fused into a continent – an almost invisible, almost imperceptible country inhabited by the zek people . . .

So it was that the word Gulag – strictly GULag, the official abbreviation in Russian for the Main Administration of Corrective Labour Camps – was launched on the English-speaking world. The date was May 1974 and the author of this 'Experiment in Literary Investigation', as *The Gulag Archipelago* was subtitled, was the ex-zek or convict Alexander Solzhenitsyn.

The original Russian edition had been published a few months ear-lier, in Paris. The text, however, had already been in the West for five years, smuggled out of Russia with the help of a Swedish journalist and friends of one of Solzhenitsyn's collaborators. All that was needed for publication was the author's word. He had delayed and delayed and for a compelling reason: publication would have jeopardized the safety, even perhaps the lives, of the 227 'witnesses' whose experiences he had drawn on for the book. What forced his hand was the seizure of a copy of the manuscript by the KGB, the Soviet secret police.

The circumstances of the seizure convey the conditions in which Solzhenitsyn and other dissident writers, and their helpers, worked. Unbeknown to the author, who thought all copies of his typescript had been smuggled out of Russia or destroyed, one of his dedicated team of typists had buried a copy in a friend's garden. In August 1973 that woman, Elizaveta Denisovna Voronyanskaya, in her sixties and in poor health, was arrested and subjected to several days of interrogation, during which she divulged the existence and whereabouts of her copy. A few weeks after her release she was found dead in the hallway of her communal apartment, hanging from a rope. It was presumed she had killed herself out of remorse. One neighbour reported, however, that the body had knife wounds and blood on it.

Solzhenitsyn now expected arrest and imprisonment himself. It would be a repeat: in 1945, serving as an army captain, he had been arrested for criticizing Stalin in a letter to a friend, interrogated in the Lubyanka jail in Moscow and given an eight-year sentence for 'anti-Soviet agitation'. Sent to a special prison to work on government projects, he was later transferred to a forced labour camp for refusing to co-operate on one of the research programmes. His experiences at the camp led to the book that brought him literary fame, *One Day in the Life of Ivan Denisovich* (1962).

Ivan Denisovich was the only major work of Solzhenitsyn's to be published in the Soviet Union and it only saw the light of day thanks to a brief easing of cultural controls under Khrushchev. When Khrushchev fell, in 1964, the 'thaw' ended and Solzhenitsyn again became an unperson, unable to publish. But the novel had been a publishing sensation in the Soviet Union. Many Russian readers were said to have wept over its pages, while some did more than weep: they wrote to its author about their own experiences, which Solzhenitsyn added to the grim historical tapestry he was stitching together in *The Gulag Archipelago*.

By the time *Gulag* was completed in 1967 Solzhenitsyn had woven together his own experiences with the testimony of 227 fellow ex-convicts – the 'witnesses'– and quotation from official Soviet publications, employed to devastating effect. A sense of the black humour and caustic irony of the style, and his bravura use of punctuation marks and italics, can be gleaned from this passage, on people's failure to resist arbitrary arrest:

Universal innocence also gave rise to the universal failure to act.

Anna Trench

Maybe they *won't take* you? Maybe it will all blow over? A. I. Ladyzhensky was the chief teacher in a school in remote Kologriv. In 1937 a peasant approached him in an open market and passed him a message from a third person: 'Aleksandr Ivanich, get out of town, *you are on the list!*' But he stayed: After all, the whole school rests on my shoulders, and *their own* children are pupils here. How can they arrest me? (Several days later he was arrested.) . . . The majority sit quietly and dare to hope. Since you aren't guilty, then how can they arrest you? *It's a mistake!* They are already dragging you along by the collar, and you still keep exclaiming to yourself: 'It's a mistake! *They'll set things straight and let me out!*' Others are being arrested en masse, and that's a bothersome fact, but in those other cases there is always some dark area: Maybe *he* was guilty . . . ?' But as for you, you are obviously innocent!

Here, where Solzhenitsyn is writing of the victims, his irony is gentler, softened by compassion; when he comes to the behaviour of high officials, such as chief public prosecutors Krylenko and Vyshinsky, his pen is dipped in acid: his withering scorn reduces once mighty and revered figures, who had occupied some of the most senior positions in the state, to the status of common criminals, uncommon only in the extent of their crimes. I still remember my sense of shock, reading the book in the 1970s, at some of the quotations:

> In the interrogation do not seek evidence and proof that the person accused acted in word or deed against Soviet power. The first questions should be: What is his class, what is his origin, what is his education and upbringing? These are the questions which must determine the fate of the accused. (M. I. Latsis, a Chekist official)
>
> Give us the body and we will produce the case. (KGB interrogator)
>
> At the Novosibirsk Transit Prison in 1945 they greeted prisoners with a roll call based on cases. 'So and so! Article 58-1a, twenty-five years.' The chief of the convoy guard was curious: 'What did you get it for?' 'For nothing at all.' '*You're lying. The sentence for nothing at all is ten years.*'

Just to marshal and organize the vast amount of material in the book – it stretches in its English edition over three volumes and 1,798 pages – was a forbidding task for any man, let alone one who had to work clandestinely, constantly moving from one friend's apartment to another, and never able to have the entire work on his desk at one time, fearing the knock on the door and the loss of years of work at one blow. But to force that material into artistic form, to thread together so many strands of individual fates, to sustain the tone of impassioned rage at the injustice and inhumanity of an entire state apparatus towards its own citizens, required the dedication and gifts of a great writer and a tough one at that. At times he was working a sixteen-hour day, in two shifts, sleeping with a pitchfork by his bed 'for self-defence if needed'.

It is hard to think of parallels in literary history to either the work itself or the circumstances of its composition. Histories combining the personal testimony of witnesses and participants with the historian's overarching narrative were rare at the time, so even formally *The Gulag Archipelago* was a revelation. But its author had not even really called it a history: it was 'An Experiment in Literary Investigation'. This odd description indicated that this was no conventional history – indeed could not be, since its writer had little or no access to any of the documentary evidence – but was an imaginative effort to depict and understand the reality, including the psychological reality, of a catastrophic but almost totally hidden chapter in his country's history.

Once published, the book made an immediate impact. Within a few weeks, extracts from the Russian version were being read on the BBC's Russian Service and other stations. When the American translation came out in May 1974, the reaction was dramatic. Earlier accounts of the evils of Stalinism had appeared in the West, but they had only dented the residual belief of many that Soviet communism represented a noble aspiration towards an ideal society – even if 'regrettable aberrations' had taken place. After *The Gulag Archipelago*, it was impossible to cling to that belief. The power of Solzhenitsyn's indictment of what he clearly regarded, and what the masses of testimony in his book demonstrated, as a criminal regime from its inception, equal or even 'superior' in murderous intent and execution to that of the Nazis, seemed to bury for good the hope that any 'perfect' society could be built along communist lines. As one commentator wrote, *The Gulag Archipelago* challenged the very foundation of the Soviet Union. The former US ambassador to Moscow George Kennan described it as 'the greatest and most powerful single indictment of a political regime ever to be levelled in modern times'.

Or possibly in any time. Seen from today's vantage point, the publication of *The Gulag Archipelago* appears like the first artillery barrage of an assault that within only two decades would bring about the collapse of the world's second superpower. Solzhenitsyn, expelled from the Soviet Union on 13 February 1974, held on to a belief, seemingly ridiculous at the time, that he would be able to return to his native Russia in his lifetime. Only sixteen years after the publication of his book, the apparently impossible happened: the Berlin Wall fell and the mighty USSR crumbled to dust before our eyes.

L. W. Webb, reviewing *The Gulag Archipelago* in May 1974, wrote: 'To live now and not to know this work is to be a kind of historical fool missing a part of the consciousness of the age.' One might think that with the demise of the Soviet system, the end of the forced-labour camps and the appearance of fuller histories, written with the aid of newly accessible documents, Solzhenitsyn's monumental work would have lost its relevance and be itself of merely historical interest. This assumption would be mistaken. One only has to pick it up and start reading to be swept back into that bleak and terrible world, carried along by the vivid power of its guide's literary (and historical) imagination:

> Rosy-fingered Eos, so often mentioned in Homer and called Aurora by the Romans, caressed, too, with those fingers the first early morning of the Archipelago . . .

After a 25-year career divided between the BBC World Service and London's Wiener Library, ANTHONY WELLS now devotes as much time to writing as running a small family business allows.

My Most Precious Book

FRANCES WILSON

In general, I'm cavalier about books. I lend them and therefore lose them, scribble in them, festoon them in pink Post-it notes, share baths with them and pile them up on shelves and tables in no particular order.

Only one book is treated differently. *Traditional Romance and Tale: How Stories Mean*, by Anne Wilson, has a shelf-space of its own on the top left-hand side of the bookcase in my study. As light as balsa wood, it comes to little more than 100 chalky pages. The index takes up one page and the cover, royal blue, has an image from the *Book of Hours* in which a young knight reads the script on a stone, while the setting sun casts shadows behind him. I love the knight's modesty, and the modesty of the book itself: the object in my house which takes up the least space carries the most weight. I would lend this book to no one; nor would I write in it or take it anywhere near hot water. *Traditional Romance and Tale* taught me how to read – not in the sense of taking me through the alphabet, but of showing me what a strange and mysterious thing reading is, how the part of the mind that absorbs itself in the structure and pattern of stories is at the same time primitive and supremely intelligent.

Anne Wilson begins with a question: why didn't the Sleeping Beauty's parents put a note in their diaries, to remind them that on her fifteenth birthday she would be pricked by a needle? What on earth were they doing, letting her wander around by herself on that day of all days? Wilson's thesis is this: many of the indestructible stories we live amongst – fairytales, folk tales, medieval romances, the *Odyssey*, *Jane Eyre* – don't make sense: 'the thinking in them is not predominantly the kind of thinking which we bring to everyday affairs'. Their thinking is closer to that of dreams, and if we search in these texts for rational meanings 'the answers to our questions will be somewhat like the answers given to Macbeth by the Weird Sisters'. Anne Wilson always makes her own meanings clear and her ideas, explored in the clean, nimble prose of a writer untainted by university life, are as fresh today as they were when the book was published in 1976.

Traditional Romance and Tale awakened me to the power of the unconscious mind, and also showed me how tough writing was. The book took years to build; like Emily Dickinson, Anne Wilson wrote from a desk in her bedroom, rarely coming downstairs. I know this because I grew up around the book's creation. It began life when I was 7 and was published when I was 12: it was my question about the Sleeping Beauty's negligent parents that my mother set out to answer in her opening chapter. Great lengths of paper hung from her wall, charting the movements of the plots she was studying. When I wondered what these labyrinthine maps meant, she explained: 'This, Frances, is how the mind works.' I would get home from school to find her asleep, exhausted from a day's thought and unravelling in her dreams – so she told me – a problem she was pursuing in *King Horn* or *Sir Gawain and the Green Knight*.

Thus I watched the book grow, from seed to full flowering, and saw my mother's disappointment when her work was initially ignored. English Departments were taken over by structuralism and deconstruction; scholarship was seen as old-school. Wordsworth praised all books which 'lay their sure foundations in the heart of man': this precious volume has provided the foundation, the heart, of my love of reading and my determination to write.

FRANCES WILSON is a critic and biographer. *Guilty Thing: An Inner Life of Thomas De Quincey* will be published by Bloomsbury later this year.

Down-to-Earth in Over Stowey

ANTHONY LONGDEN

I have always had a weakness for diaries and memoirs, especially those written by men of the cloth. It's generally quite gentle observational stuff, cataloguing the daily round, usually in a country parish, and much of its fascination lies in the diurnal detail, some of it joyous, some of it poignant, as local characters are christened, married and buried. This writing, for me at least, provides an instant escape to a lost world running at less than half the speed of our own.

The varying styles are always individual. Dear old Parson James Woodforde of Norfolk begins his diary in October 1758 with some entries made when he was at Oxford, giving an interesting insight into the life of an undergraduate at the time. He lists various purchases such as 'a pair of Curling Tongs', 'Two Logick Books', 'Two Bottles of Port Wine' and 'A New Wigg', and goes on to give us a wealth of wonderful impressions of domestic life – receiving deliveries from a smuggler for tea, 'a Tub of Gin' or 'the best Coniac Brandy', dining with a bewildering range of relatives, friends and parishioners, and tackling all manner of servant problems.

The diary of the Reverend Francis Edward Witts is notable mainly because he saw the rapid development of late Georgian Cheltenham at first hand, but it is also paralyzingly dull in places:

> January 3, 1820: Left Upper Slaughter for Bath in the hope that another course of the waters may essentially strengthen my dear

Jack Ayres (ed.), *Paupers and Pig Killers: The Diary of William Holland, A Somerset Parson, 1799–1818*, first published by Alan Sutton in 1984, is out of print.

wife's constitution. Having sent forward my manservant and horse we travelled with Edward and a maid. The weather very cold, frost and snow . . .

Then there are the pompous and self-regarding, the Reverend Benjamin John Armstrong of Norfolk among them:

September 14, 1850: Having this day been instituted by the Bishop of Norwich to the Vicarage of East Dereham, with the perpetual curacy of Hoe annexed, it becomes my duty to give some account of a place which, with God's blessing, is to be the scene of my future labours.

And, of course, there is the gentle, compelling prose of the Reverend Francis Kilvert, who opened his diary on 8 February 1870 with this:

From Wye Cliff to Pont Faen. Miss Child in great force. She showed me her clever drawings of horses and told me the adventures of the brown wood owl 'Ruth' which she took home from here last year. She wanted to call the owl 'Eve' but Mrs Bridge said it should be called 'Ruth'.

But by far and away my favourite is the Reverend William Holland, a gloriously feisty and choleric cleric who reaches out from the page and seizes you roughly by the lapels right from the beginning:

Wednesday, October 23, 1799: Went with my wife to Stowey and she bought a gown of Mr Frank Poole who smiled and bowed graciously. Saw that Democratic hoyden Mrs Coleridge who looked so like a friskey girl or something worse that I was not surprised that a Democratic Libertine should choose her for a wife. The husband gone to London suddenly, no one here can tell why. Met the patron of the democrats, Mr Thos

Poole who smiled and chatted a little. He was on his gray mare, Satan himself cannot be more false and hypocritical.

Holland is a man who speaks his mind. He has no time for idleness, pretension, vanity, drunkenness, unreliability or anything else on the long list of human frailties he regularly encounters in his Somerset parish of Over Stowey, on the edge of the ruggedly beautiful Quantock Hills.

I was introduced to this incendiary personality thanks to a 1995 Alan Sutton paperback with the irresistible title: *Paupers and Pig Killers: The Diary of William Holland, A Somerset Parson, 1799–1818.* The quote is one of Holland's own – an unflinching assessment of his parishioners. But then he wasn't a local. He was an incomer, a Welshman, born in Teyrdan, Denbighshire, in May 1746, and could trace his family roots back to John Holland, Duke of Exeter, who died in 1446.

Holland graduated from Jesus College, Oxford, in 1768, and began his career as a curate at Cherington in Worcestershire. He stayed there only a short while, moving next to the grand church of St Mary's, Reading, and then to Over Stowey on 3 September 1779. In 1786, he took on the additional living of Monkton Farleigh, near Bath, and held both until his death on 17 April 1819.

The sheer joy of his diary is that you can plunge in anywhere in the certainty of finding a gem.

Monday, October 28, 1799: A great bustle – Wm Frost and Mr Amen carrying apples to the cart for cyder. They are taken down to Hewlett's to be made through his hair cloths which is not the fashion of this county. Mr Amen thinks it is impossible for the cyder to be good as it is not made after the fashion of the county. I tell him he is a blockhead and that he knows nothing of the matter. 'Why Sir, I have made hundreds of hogsheads of cyder in my time.' 'Silence you Ass.'

Holland calls all Parish Clerks 'Amen' or 'Mr Amen', and he is seldom impressed by their efforts. Nor is he particularly tolerant of Democrats, Methodists, Catholics or a host of other religious groupings.

Thursday, October 31: Mr Hurley is to send me a bag of red potatoes. Tho' an Anabaptist I do not dislike the man for he seems to be a fair dealer. I wish all Sectarians were like him for in general I have found them full of malice, ignorant, narrow minded and void of either candour or charity.

And while Kilvert would spend time on easy-flowing descriptions of the countryside around Clyro, or the beauty of some of its young women, Holland is prosaic.

Monday, November 11: Briffet is here to kill the sow. A horrible looking fellow, his very countenance is sufficient to kill anything, a large hulky fellow, a face absolutely furrowed with the small pox (a very uncommon thing in these days of inoculations), two ferret eyes and a little turned up nose with a mouth as wide as a barn door and lips as thick, and projecting they look like two rollers of raw beef bolstered up to guard against, as it were, the approach to his nasty ragged rotten teeth. However he is a good pig killer.

These were turbulent times for the country, and Holland had a keen interest in current affairs, eagerly awaiting the arrival of his daily newspaper. He frequently misspells 'Buonaparte', whom he loathed with a passion.

Thursday, November 21, 1799: A great Revolution once more in France, that rascal Beunoparte is returned from Egypt having stolen away from the Army and left 'em to Old Nick.
Sunday, October 5, 1800: The newspaper come. Malta has surrendered to the British Arms, Huzza.

Infuriatingly, Holland's notebooks for the period April 1814 – October 1815 are missing, so we will never know precisely what he made of the defeat of 'Bonnypart' at Waterloo, although it is perhaps easy to guess.

Next, he focuses on America.

Monday, January 1, 1816: The Year has been eventful for and Victorious for Great Britain and the Peace founded on Justice and Honour and Religion and she is universally acknowledged to be the First Empire in the World. But her former Colonies in America, tho' now at Peace with her are still full of Envy and Malice against her and ready to join in any scheme for her destruction, tho' she has been their Saviour, evidently from the Dominion of Buonaparte who has now a strong party among them.

It would be a mistake, however, to dismiss Holland merely as an irascible, uncaring man. There is much evidence in the diary of a deep attachment to the people in his charge, even if they frequently failed to meet his own high standards. Country parishes in the late eighteenth century had more than their fair share of challenges. Holland raged in one entry about the 'disgusting' behaviour of a man who had made his daughter pregnant. The child was later still-born, but Holland repeatedly said he wanted to see the man brought to justice. That justice came soon enough when a fever carried the miscreant off.

Death was ever present. 'Sunday, August 24, 1800: A great many persons at Asholt. There was a burying and a christening there. The father buried and his child christened on the same day, 'twas a melancholy circumstance. He has left nine children, many of them small.' Holland himself had known tragedy. In 1795 there was a serious outbreak of scarlet fever. His five children all fell ill, and within just two weeks four were dead. Only his daughter, Mary, survived.

The couple were blessed with a new arrival in 1797, baby William, who remained the apple of his father's eye. We see Mary and William grow up in the pages of the diaries, and the story of the Holland family has no further tragic twists.

Overall, I think Holland did his best. The life of the incumbent of a small country parish like Over Stowey was simple enough – one Sunday service a week, visiting the sick, conducting marriages, christenings and funerals. It was, and remains bleak, dank and atmospheric country, a geographical cul-de-sac, certainly not a destination. These days, the area is dominated by the nuclear power station at Hinkley Point, the visitor's view on the way to the coast here frequently interrupted by plaits of power cables hitched to huge metal pylons striding across the fields. And yet it is a fertile place. The Holland household was able to be largely self-sufficient, the vicarage having around eight acres at its disposal. There were stables, a barn and a yard, and the vicar kept horses, pigs and cattle. Vegetables were grown, bread baked, and beer and cider brewed. Any surplus was given to the poor.

We know from the diary that the Hollands employed a cook/maid and were also 'helped' by a man-of-all-work who would do everything from mucking out the animals and digging the vegetable patch to going on errands and even serving at table. Holland got through quite a few of these. They seldom measured up, and his mounting dissatisfaction frequently found an outlet through his pen, so providing us with some of the most amusing passages in the diary.

In addition to his interest in current affairs, Holland also carefully recorded the readings from his thermometer and barometer. Such was the ferocity of the winters, he sometimes refers to the room being so cold his fingers were numb and unable to grip the pen.

In the fruitful seasons, the comparative plenty of the vicarage garden was not lost on some of his neighbours.

Sunday, August 31, 1800: Before Church this evening in going to the bottom of the garden I perceived the plum tree moving and a person's head above the hedge. I called out and ran to the place but he was off, yet I secured the article of depredation, a strong hook, which he must have prepared for the purpose with some pains and care. It was a neighbour's son, Charles Sellick's son, a great looby from seventeen to eighteen years of age. It is hard to be plundered by one's neighbours who receive so many favours at our hands. I told the father of it.

Holland's diary originally consisted of ninety notebooks, but some have been lost. My Alan Sutton paperback features a picture of a page from one of them. It reveals strong, educated handwriting with a pronounced rightward slant, the lines all drifting upwards, clearly written at some speed. Jack Ayres, who edited *Paupers and Pig Killers*, believes Holland would still have retained his Welsh accent, and I think you can hear that in the entries, especially the angrier ones.

It is surprising Holland isn't better known. He gives us glimpses of simple lives lived in a very quiet corner of an increasingly turbulent world and a charmingly flawed narrator, but one whose heart was in the right place.

ANTHONY LONGDEN is a journalist, media consultant and former newspaper editor.

The Dean and the Don

DEREK PARKER

Back in 1968, when I was editing *Poetry Review*, published by the Poetry Society, I started a campaign to have a memorial to Byron placed in Poets' Corner. I was tentative in my first approach to the Dean and Chapter of Westminster Abbey, suspecting they might not be particularly enthusiastic about giving space to a man who boasted of having enjoyed a hundred different women during his first two years in Venice and who thought that 'all sense and senses' were against belief in religion.

Fortunately the Dean at the time was Eric Abbott, a highly culti-vated and intelligent man who sympathized when I pointed out that at the very least Byron *sought* to believe, even if he found it as diffi-cult as 'walking in the dark over a rabbit warren – or a garden with steel traps and spring guns'. But confessing he knew little of the poetry, the Dean asked me what he should read to convince him that Byron was indeed a great poet. I steered him determinedly towards *Don Juan*. Within a month, he had persuaded the Chapter to give permission, with the support of the Poetry Society the funds were raised, and William Plomer eventually unveiled the stone in the floor of Poets' Corner.

We don't read long poems these days, more's the pity. Yet they are often wonderful achievements, and by restricting ourselves to popu-lar extracts we do ourselves a disservice. But I must not sound like the preacher Byron once heard, who leaned from the pulpit and

Don Juan can be found in Lord Byron, *The Major Works* · OUP · Pb · 1,120pp · £12.99 · ISBN 9780199537334.

exclaimed: 'No hopes for them as *laughs*.' The cure for those who think long poems unreadable and necessarily dull is – as the good Dean found – a dose of *Don Juan*.

It was that earlier long poem *Childe Harold's Pilgrimage* that legendarily made Byron famous overnight. He started *Juan* six years later, in 1818, and I really think originally for his own amusement rather than very obviously for publication – even he thought it perhaps 'too free for these very modest days'; and indeed publication of each of the seventeen cantos was dogged by difficulty: Murray, Byron's publisher, was horrified by the 'approximations to indelicacy' in the poem, and the poet again and again complained of his attempts to censor it by 'damned cutting & slashing'. Very few readers were offended: most were delighted by the liveliest and most readable, wittiest and most acerbic poem of its time.

Byron said that *Don Juan* was meant to be 'a little quietly facetious about everything'. He went on writing it, on and off, for the rest of his life, sometimes at breakneck speed, sometimes at odd moments – even after falling into a Venetian canal from the balcony of a lady with whom he had no doubt been discussing the poetry of Wordsworth, he sat down still shivering to add a couple of stanzas. He showed no sign of ever wanting to end it, aiming to send Juan to most of the countries of Europe in order to satirize national traits; he 'had not quite fixed whether to make him end in Hell, or in an unhappy marriage, not knowing which would be the severest'.

The poem has nothing to do with the Don Juan of Spanish origin, who appears in Mozart's *Don Giovanni* and elsewhere; not even the same pronunciation, being for rhyming purposes pronounced *Jew-un*. Byron's Juan isn't really a womanizer – just a man easily seduced, and it has to be admitted that attempted and often successful seduction does play a large part in the poem: love is treated as satirically as everything else. *Don Juan* is almost a versified *Tom Jones*, as lively and vigorous and full of fun as Fielding's novel. In the first canto Juan is hiding from a suspicious husband in the very bedclothes of the wife; Cantos II–IV provide a halcyon and tender love story with a tragic ending – but in Canto V we find Juan bought by a sultan's wife for her male harem. And so it goes – Juan as a 'favourite' of Catherine II of Russia, cutting a swathe through the fashionable ladies of London . . . If it all sounds pretty flippant, so it is; but it's a sublime flippancy.

Some of the lines will certainly be familiar to those who have never opened the poem:

> A little still she strove, and much repented
> And whispering 'I will ne'er consent' – consented.

> Man's love is of man's life a thing apart,
> 'Tis woman's whole existence.

> What men call gallantry, and gods adultery,
> Is much more common where the climate's sultry.

There are many, many more acute aphorisms: 'Ready money is Aladdin's lamp' or 'Wrinkles, the damned democrats, won't flatter' – but also occasionally stanzas of real passion, when for instance he writes of Greece and the war with the Turks in which he was to participate and die. But he couldn't be serious for long, always ready to puncture a posture with a joke:

B. Lodge

But I digress: of all appeals, – although
I grant the power of pathos, and of gold,
Of beauty, flattery, threats, a shilling, – no
Method's more sure at moments to take hold
Of the best feelings of mankind, which grow
More tender, as we every day behold,
Than that all-softening, overpowering knell,
The tocsin of the soul – the dinner-bell.

I have to say, the longer I live the more pleased I am to have succeeded in convincing Dean Abbott to place what I suppose was the first Abbey memorial to commemorate a confirmed agnostic (there have been many since); and the more happy I am to adhere to my hero's advice on life and how to live it –

Let us have wine and women, mirth and laughter,
Sermons and soda water the day after.

DEREK PARKER's *Byron: The Impossible Hero* is available to download from Kindle or Amazon.

Gaiety and Magic

RICHARD DAVIES

Perhaps some of the best moments in a book-lover's life are when you chance upon something that turns out to be a real find. The first of many such discoveries for me was a well-used Penguin entitled *Twenty Years A-Growing*, which I came across nearly sixty years ago, in the back room of a junk shop. I bought it for a penny, read the whole book that day and loved every word of it. I have it still and often revisit it.

First published in 1933, the book is a lively and lyrical account by Maurice O'Sullivan of his early years on the island of Great Blasket in the far west of Ireland – so far west, indeed, that the church in Dunquin, the nearest town on the mainland that served the island's needs, had listed as its closest parish to the west 'Boston, America'.

It tells of a life of virtual subsistence in a hard place, where the weather, the money earned from selling mackerel and lobsters on the mainland, and the treasures to be found on the beaches should a ship founder at sea dictated the pace of life. The outside world could only be reached by rowing across two and a half miles of open sea in a curragh, a flimsy coracle made of wood and tarred canvas. A hard place, yes, but also one of freedom and adventure. To me as a small boy living in suburban North London it seemed a paradise.

Great Blasket's inhabitants burned turf for fuel and ate everything from fish and mutton to puffins pulled from holes in the ground and thrushes caught in caves at Hallowe'en. They even scaled sheer cliffs

Maurice O'Sullivan, *Twenty Years A-Growing* (1933)
OUP · Pb · 320pp · £7.50 · ISBN 9780192813251

to look for gulls' eggs. There were whales and porpoises in the sea and huge flocks of gulls and other seabirds on the rocky cliffs.

For entertainment they made music, danced and listened to stories in the original Gaelic recounted by old men and women, often illiterate, who had heard them at the feet of their forebears and had committed them to memory. It was a place largely untouched by the outside world.

At the start of the book O'Sullivan writes:

> I am a boy who was born and bred in the Great Blasket, a small truly Gaelic island which lies north-west of the coast of Kerry, where the storms of the sky and the wild sea beat against the wrinkled rocks which stand above the waves that wash in and out of the coves where the seals make their homes.

This sets the scene for an exuberant account of life in a world that has now vanished. It is a story full of adventure, drama and laughter. In one splendid chapter Maurice and his friend Tomas spend a day at the Ventry curragh races – a

Nathan Ariss

wonderful boyish romp described with verve and humour. In another he and his father are fishing in their curragh when it is nearly swamped by a whale that surfaces beside them. Maurice recalls vividly the stink of the whale's breath and how he fears he will have to throw his much-loved dog, which is in the boat with him, into the sea to distract the giant creature as they row desperately to safety.

My favourite of these tales, though, is the description of how Maurice, going into a crowded pub on the mainland to find his father and brothers after a wedding, bends down to retrieve his cap which has fallen to the floor and is unable to get up again because a big man standing alongside will not move. 'As he gave me no heed I got angry, so that when I found on the floor a pin sharply pointed I thrust it into his thigh.' The man kicked out in pain and struck the man in front of him who spilled his beer and fell to the floor. A huge fight ensued and as Maurice slipped away he saw 'blood flying to the rafters and some foolish fellow encouraging the man from whom it was flowing, shouting, "Your soul to the devil, don't let down City-cow-titty. Remember your ancestors! Strike the bostoon!"'

The story of how the book came to be written is equally fascinating. Great Blasket was of interest to scholars because it was one of the last places in Ireland where Gaelic was still the common language, and the islanders had retained their oral folklore. One of these academics, an English classicist called George Thomson, befriended the 19-year-old Maurice while on a visit in 1923, persuaded him to write his story and arranged for it to be translated into English. Thomson also asked E. M. Forster to write a foreword to the book in which the novelist said: 'All this – both the gaiety and the magic – can be sampled in the opening chapter, and the reader can decide for himself quickly, so that there is no need to say to him "this book is good".'

Forster thought the book described 'a neolithic civilization from the inside' and that the author 'keeps our world in its place and views it only from his place'. He's right: there is an other-worldly quality about the life of the islanders surviving against huge odds while the wider world rarely intrudes. When it does – as when they find the washed-up body of an officer from the *Lusitania*, torpedoed off the Irish coast by a German submarine in 1915 – the difference is stark. And when steam trawlers arrive in their waters, literally to hoover up the fish the islanders depend upon for their livelihood, reality bites hard.

As the old way of life crumbles, the younger inhabitants turn their thoughts to emigration. For many the dream of travelling to America becomes a reality. They leave by curragh to go to Dingle where they catch the train to Cork and then a ship that will take them across the Atlantic. In time it is only the old men and women who are left.

Maurice's departure from the island was of a different order. Not for him a new life in America. Instead he went to Dublin to join the Police, the Garda Siochana. His journey was not exactly without drama though: he managed to team up with a brother and sister who were also going to the capital and relied on them to show him the way. He little knew that the boy was as ignorant of the route as he was and they ended up in Cork.

He made it to Dublin eventually, was looked after by Thomson and stayed with Moya Llewellyn Davies, who was to become the translator of *Twenty Years A-Growing*. For the first time in his life he saw street lights and motor cars, visited a cinema and enjoyed the luxury of indoor plumbing. He duly passed the Garda selection board and in 1927 was posted to Connemara, where he would eventually make his home. His book was published to great acclaim in 1933. In 1950, aged 46, he tragically drowned while swimming in the sea with his family.

In 1953 the last inhabitant of Great Blasket left the island and it has been uninhabited ever since. One or two cottages have been restored so that descendants of emigrants can return and get a taste of the life their forefathers led, but the rest are in ruins.

There are other books about the Blasket by men and women who grew up there, written under the auspices of other academics. But for me *Twenty Years A-Growing* remains the best of them. O'Sullivan wrote it for those who knew him and his home, not for a wider audience. It is this that gives it the elusive quality of what Forster called 'gaiety and magic'.

RICHARD DAVIES is busy rewriting his self-published novel *After Adlestrop* with the encouragement of a real publisher. He has also put together a slim volume of his poetry for family and friends.

Behind the Net Curtains

SARAH CROWDEN

The maxim 'write what you know' has been drummed into aspiring novelists on creative writing courses for years and it aptly sums up the varied career of R. F. Delderfield, whose writing life was divided into three distinct parts. He was encouraged early on by George Bernard Shaw and Graham Greene among others, and one of his several mentors advised him to 'write what pleases you and you have a slim chance of pleasing others by accident'.

R. F. (Ron) Delderfield was 6 when in 1918 his family, shaken by the Great War's air raids, moved, as so many Cockney families did, to the suburbs. Ashburton Avenue, Addiscombe was then on the Kent/Surrey border, close to Shirley, an outer London 'ring', near Croydon – very different from Bermondsey and a paradise for a small boy. Five years later, his father upped sticks to Devon, changed his job and became editor of a weekly local paper, the *Exmouth Chronicle*, where Delderfield worked after leaving boarding-school as a reporter and 'virtual sub-editor'. He interviewed visiting celebrities, wrote memorial notices (an inappropriate source of hilarity), attended weddings and funerals, and was required to fold the papers prior to distribution. Though his father considered him fortunate to have a job in the late 1920s when unemployment was widespread, Delderfield felt his prospects were limited, and he determined to write a successful play.

R. F. Delderfield, *The Dreaming Suburb* (1958), is available as a Hodder paperback (480pp · £8.99 · ISBN 9780340963760). *The Avenue Goes to War* (1958) is out of print.

Returning to London, he worked his way through the *Writers' and Artists' Yearbook* and was on the cusp of success when war broke out again. Having been rejected for training as air-crew because of his extreme short-sightedness, he joined up as a clerk and did unpaid stage writing for the RAF (including a pantomime). He eventually joined the bomb disposal squad since he was considered insufficiently educated to be an officer. The armed forces would prove to be a rich source of copy.

Discharged in 1945, he was delighted to discover that a play he had sent to several theatres years earlier and forgotten about had been picked up. *Worm's Eye View*, described by its first producer as 'on the face of it, a farcical comedy of low genre', became a huge success, eventually transferring to the West End where it became a popular fixture. Delderfield's father looked upon his son's dramatic endeavours with a jaundiced eye, and only went to the play more than halfway through its five-year run after 'the local pork butcher . . . assured him that it was well worth seeing'.

In 1956, disillusioned with the theatre, Delderfield gave it up, began to write novels and 'at once put on weight'. He found he was far happier with his characters 'safely imprisoned between two hard covers and not in a position to dispute their exits and entrances' – unlike the actors and actresses in his plays, who clearly drove him to distraction. He was also a reasonably successful screenwriter, but never made much of television, though after he died, aged 60 in 1972, many of his novels were adapted for the small screen and were avidly watched by huge audiences throughout the 1970s and early '80s. Among these was the Avenue series, retitled *People like Us*.

Published in 1958 and located, like Delderfield's childhood home, near Croydon, in the lightly fictionalized 'Manor Park Avenue', the two Avenue novels tell of the daily life of a suburban community. They are a robust defence of suburban life, its values, its architecture and its residents, 'who dream as extravagantly as anyone else', impervious to the sneers and derision of those who despise suburbia and all it stands for, though Delderfield does skewer their weaknesses and occasional pretensions.

The Avenue books were the first of his enormously successful 'sagas'. *The Dreaming Suburb* covers the years 1919 to 1940, and its sequel, *The Avenue Goes to War*, 1940 to 1947. Five families are introduced, four on the 'even' side of the Avenue, one on the 'odd'. The largest (seven in all) is that of the Carvers at No. 20, father Jim a widower, recently returned from the trenches. Next door at No. 22 live Esme Fraser and his mother Eunice, trailing her lovelorn solicitor and eventual spouse Harold Godbeer in her wake. It is Harold who personifies the suburban mindset – fussy, correct and resistant to change, at the opposite end of the political spectrum from Jim Carver.

For Esme, as for Delderfield, the open countryside so close to the houses is a revelation. Local landmarks feature in the books, and Delderfield uses them to good effect – the cinema, the 'rec' where lovers' trysts are made and broken, and the annual Fair on the Shirley Hills. Then there's the Avenue itself, the houses ('some . . . had names as well as numbers') with stained-glass panels in the front doors, a porch bedroom window where goings-on are observed, and chain-link fences dividing the properties at the front.

At No. 4 live the spinster Clegg sisters: Becky, the younger, has a 'past' and a mental age of 7, and they exist in genteel poverty until they find a lodger, Ted, who epitomizes the age with his passion for jazz and his extensive knowledge (like the author's) of 1920s sheet music. Edith Clegg loves the cinema as fervently as her creator did, and much of her dialogue on the subject could have been his.

A lovely description in the first book of 'the summer evening orchestra of the suburbs, the low, pleasant whine of lawn-mowers, the chink of watering-can and spade . . . and the metallic snick-snack of hand-shears, hard at work on unruly privet' evokes the continuity of suburban life, while within the houses passions seethe and some residents plot their escape. This parochial existence is lived against the background of historical events such as the General Strike (most of which leave the Avenue dwellers, with their 'pitifully limited horizons of thought', unaffected). Central London, only twelve miles away, might as well be another country. But the outbreak of war brings seismic changes, and people's dreams go into cold storage for five years. Characters leave, most to join up, but their stories are followed, and their adventures always lead them back to the Avenue. In occupied France, Esme meets a man who once lived round the corner.

In *The Avenue Goes to War*, which opens in mid-1940, Delderfield kills off a total of seventeen Avenue residents but is unable to bring himself to kill Bernard Carver who, with his twin brother Boxer, provide much of the comedy in the novels – first as naughty boys, then as fearless Commandos. Even the most conventional resident, Edith Clegg, breaks out in her own small way. The Avenue loses its pre-war trimness and many of its occupants lose their insularity. Ted the lodger, now married, quite literally experiences a sea-change after meeting a refugee from the concentration camps, and feels he must do his bit.

Jim and Harold forge an unlikely friendship, both agreeing that they've 'got to face up to things as a *people* again, the way we did last time'. The conflict creeps closer to home with bombing raids destroying the symmetry of the Avenue, while the quiet humdrum lives its residents once enjoyed disappear. Those who return find an Avenue irrevocably changed. It still has its values, and its residents still have their dreams, but they are different now.

I won't spoil the experience for anyone reading the books for the first time by going into more detail. Suffice to say that it is definitely a case of *amor vincit omnia*. At the end of *The Avenue Goes to War* we find Jim Carver, now 67, still disillusioned by politicians, yet grudgingly optimistic, having discovered that it is friends that matter most – 'energetic, steadfast, large-hearted and brave as lions'. What is left of Manor Park Avenue's 'scimitar curve' will soon be swallowed up in a tangle of new avenues, 'no longer a salient, marking the furthest advance of south-eastern London . . . just another road'.

In 1990, as a new (albeit ancient) bride, I left a wild single life in Camden, NW1, to join my husband in New Malden, Surrey – on the same latitude as Shirley and swiftly christened 'The Gateway to the Suburbs'. After the commuters had departed, there were, at that time, only two trains an hour 'up to London'. The High Street had no franchises at all, but it did have a department store which had stocked maid's uniforms up until quite recently. The place had, as expected, an air of repressed gentility. Immune to New Malden's charms until I joined the local Horticultural Society (President, Mr Pink; Secretary, Mr Broadoak), I then discovered a flair for jam-making and flower-arranging which has stood me in good stead, and an insatiable reading habit developed on those wretched off-peak trains which took forty-five minutes to reach The Smoke.

Delderfield bade an affectionate farewell to his Avenue and went on to write numerous novels and other sagas based on the people and places he knew and loved. An inaccurate biography of him was published a few years ago, but, as always, it's more rewarding to turn to the novels to understand the man. Of these, I have just eighteen to go.

SARAH CROWDEN now lives in Stepford, a south-west London suburb better known to cartographers as Wimbledon.

James B. W. Lewis

More Capability Brown

RICHARD MABEY

I like to think we run an open-door policy in our library at home in Norfolk. That is to say, on warm days in summer the door to the garden is actually open. Anyone's welcome to come in for a browse. Last summer a stoat wandered in, peered dismissively at the modest shelf of my own titles, sniffed about under my desk and then ambled out. Most Julys the house ants – here long before us and so given due respect – pour out from alarming new holes in the floor, march along the tops of my editions of Gilbert White's *Natural History of Selborne*, and shuffle in a lost and desultory way about the carpet, seeming uninterested in getting outdoors for their nuptial flights. But while I fret about the continuance of their ancient lineage, the culling is already under way. Next through the door come the bolder blackbirds and robins, hoovering the insects up in front of the shelves.

I think it's entirely proper that the place is a working natural habitat, the word library emerging from the Latin *liber*, which described a bit of bark inscribed with letters, and having secondary meanings to do with the liberties of the marketplace. A collection of books begins, I guess, as a kind of landscape. You plan its geological layers, cliffs, niches, ante-chambers. Hillocks and book-quakes erupt where the mass gets critical. And your Organizing System is probably more Capability Brown than Dewey Decimal. Inside this, as I'm sure is true with all booklovers, the whole house becomes 'landskipp'd'.

In our sixteenth-century farmhouse fiction and poetry reside chiefly in the living-room, some in a disused open hearth. Children's books are halfway up the stairs. An entirely irrational combination of dictionaries and field guides and American non-fiction swarm in a room in the one-time outhouse that I use as an office. Almost every-thing else lives in what I have rather grandly called 'the library'. In here I try to keep a semblance of order by arranging technical and academic books under subjects, and others alphabetically under author, on the dubious assumption that this ordering will mesh bet-ter with my memory. One writer I know arranges her travel books in order of the mean temperature of the region they're set in.

And this is the point, needless to say, where the library ceases to have the immemorial structure of a landscape and edges towards the rampant wildness of an ecosystem, with an agenda of its own. An old bibliophile's saw is that if you gaze at the spines of your books for long enough, you absorb the contents by a kind of chiromancy. I'm increasingly finding I have to gaze at the spines just to locate them. Pattern recognition, an entomologist would call it. I can never remember either the title or the authors of *The Garden, the Ark, the Tower and the Temple: Biblical Metaphors of Knowledge in Early Modern Europe*, but I can always find it because it is edged with a dis-tinctive pale-blue mottle of Edenic animals and plants, and lives high in the canopy (how apt that 'leaves' are common to both books and boskiness). And for all one's high intentions, orderliness seems to be wilfully disrupted by unintended and provocative conjunctions. It needed no intervention to make the philosopher and foxhunter Roger Scruton's unimpeachably conservative memoir *News from Somewhere* (in which he marries a girl 'whom I had seen poised aloft in Beaufort colours – like a painted angel in a frame') stand in mis-chievous dialectic next to Alfred Schmidt's severe *The Concept of Nature in Marx*. But I have no recollection of slightly tweaking the authorial alphabet so that David Hendy's *Noise: A Human History of Sound and Listening* sits serendipitously adjacent to Adam Gopnik's lyrical essays on Winter, with their description of the hiss and spark of Wordsworth's Lake District skating. The library is having ideas here before I do.

But it's the seasons of migration that really throw the wild card

Daniel Macklin

into the packed shelves. When I'm on a big project, I usually ferry a week's worth of likely reference sources from their various winter quarters over to where I do the actual writing. So armfuls of paper, from thin downloaded journal articles to eighteenth-century folios, cross parts of the garden like herds of wildebeest, and are set down in the library. There's no room for them of course, so they go on the floor in strange rows and clusters that I have never glimpsed just so before.

Just at the moment I am, for a book on plants and the imagination, trying to make sense of the relation between biological mimicry and literary metaphor (both cases of 'this stands for that'). The line of immediately pertinent texts is bookended by a heavy-framed Richard Cartwright painting of a white whale swimming in a black sea under a white cloud. The title at one end is Colonel Godfrey's classic 1933 monograph, *Native British Orchidaceae* – the only book I have seen where the dedication page is dominated by a photograph of the dedicatee, Godfrey's beloved late wife Hilda, posed amid the foliage in her garden. At the other is William Anderson's *The Green Man* (rather archly sub-titled 'An Archetype of our Oneness with the Earth') and I ponder, prompted by their proximity, whether Hilda was a kind of Green Woman, and the degree to which foliated hybrids permeate our imaginations.

This row, in ecological jargon, would be called a 'guild', a set of organisms that all fill similar roles or do analogous jobs. Trees that grow in swamps form a guild. So do insects with a taste for carrion. My current books are a guild in that they are all loyally devoted to a single purpose – helping me get this chapter sorted. But they are also, ecologically speaking, an 'association', a community of species which live together in one place, usually in some kind of mutually beneficial relationship. The insects, plants, fungi and bacteria that make up a termite mound comprise an association.

Groups of books, often for entirely sentimental reasons, have been taken out of the library's chaotic but well-meant order and encouraged to associate. I have one small bookcase – more ant-hill than termite condominium – entirely devoted to the works of John Clare and Ronald Blythe. I thought they would be happy together not only because Ronnie has been such a champion of and prolific writer about Clare, but because they both grant huge significance to the places where things dwell – and what principle is more important in a library? One of the choicer items in the Blythe section is an inscribed edition of the lecture he delivered at the Royal Society of Arts' Nobel Symposium in 1980, entitled 'An Inherited Perspective'.

In it he describes his shock at glimpsing John Clare's village of Helpston from an express train, 'first the platform name, and then the niggard features of one of the most essential native landscapes in English literature'. He had not even realized it was on a railway line.

Margaret Grainger's collection of *The Natural History Prose Writing of John Clare* (1983) quotes his graphic and curmudgeonly account of the sixteen species of wild orchid that grew round Helpston. Denouncing botanical science as the 'Dark System', swatting aside even the Bard himself, he proclaims the natural *rightness* of vernacular names: 'let the commentators of Shakspear say what they will nay shakspear himself has no authority for me in this particular the vulgar wereever I have been know them by [these names] only & the vulgar are always the best glossary to such things'. What emerges is not just a lexicon of popular names but a vivid list of the orchid's *addresses*. The early marsh-orchid, one of Clare's 'cuckoo buds', was 'very plentiful before the Enclosure on a Spot called Parker's Moor near Peasfield-hedge & on Deadmoor near Sneef green & Rotten moor by Moorclose but these places are now all under the plow'.

Clare is by no means the only writer to have 'named' and ascribed the identity of a plant by its dwelling-place. When Wordsworth's famous 'Primrose of the Rock', once an anchor in his Lakeland life, had degenerated into a banal religious symbol, his sister Dorothy nailed it firmly back to earth in her subtitle for William's final verses on the flower: 'Written in March 1829 on seeing a Primrose-tuft of flowers flourishing in the chink of a rock in which that Primrose tuft had been seen by us to flourish for twenty nine seasons'. The great Romantic scholar Professor Lucy Newlyn thinks that 'such elaborate specificity suggests she saw the poem as belonging to the "Inscription" genre, normally used to commemorate connections between people and places'. I first had contact with Lucy when she sent me a copy of her delightful paper on literary glowworms, which should by rights be living close to the book from which I have just quoted, *William and Dorothy Wordsworth: All in Each Other* (2013), but which for reasons of its own, has migrated to the outhouse, and a sub-sub-section of 'special gifts' . . .

You may begin to see where I am going in this round-the-bushes digression. Inscriptions, connections, authors, places – all prime librarious issues. Back in the book room the real problem comes when those briefly privileged titles have to go back 'where they belong'. Some hope. They've acquired new acquaintances, new guild partners, so their belonging has become a serious existential problem. Frankly, I'm often tempted to give up any pretence of order, and arrange the whole lot by free association, so that the library would become a leaf-space as vivaciously mobile as a rainforest. I'd never find anything I wanted, but just imagine the new symbioses and connectivities I'd discover, by – to only marginally misuse the term for what drives evolution – natural selection.

RICHARD MABEY is currently finishing *Efflorescence. The Cabaret of Plants* on a Visiting Fellowship at Cambridge, and is rationing himself to six titles in his room at a time 'so that I get thirsty for oases'.

Bibliography

Robert Aickman, *Dark Entries; Cold Hand in Mine; The Unsettled Dust; The Wine-Dark Sea*   7

Jack Ayres (ed.), *Paupers and Pig Killers: The Diary of William Holland, A Somerset Parson*   68

Mary Borden, *The Forbidden Zone*   44

Lord Byron, *Don Juan*   75

R. F. Delderfield, *The Dreaming Suburb; The Avenue Goes to War*   83

Louise Fitzhugh, *Harriet the Spy*   55

Foxe's Book of Martyrs   33

Robin Jenkins, *The Cone-Gatherers*   23

Patrick McGrath, *Asylum*   18

Gavin Maxwell, *The House of Elrig*   12

David Nobbs, *The Death of Reginald Perrin; The Return of Reginald Perrin; The Better World of Reginald Perrin*   50

Maurice O'Sullivan, *Twenty Years A-Growing*   79

Alexander Solzhenitsyn, *The Gulag Archipelago*   59

John Updike, *Rabbit, Run; Rabbit Redux; Rabbit Is Rich; Rabbit at Rest*   27

Ronald Welch, *Escape from France; Nicholas Carey*   39

Anne Wilson, *Traditional Romance and Tale*   66

All four engravings on our bookplates are by Howard Phipps: (*top*) A green lane, Exmoor; (*left*) A beech-shaded hollow, Cranborne Chase; (*centre*) Water meadow from a garden doorway; (*right*) Coombe Bissett Down

Slightly Foxed bookplates are works of art
in their own right

Actual size
110 x 80mm

EX LIBRIS
Richard Jones

EX LIBRIS
Briony and
Duncan Paterson

EX LIBRIS
Marie-Clotilde Dufriche
Desgenettes

EX LIBRIS
Elizabeth Kaye

Coming attractions . . .

RICHARD HOLLOWAY conquers his fear of Virginia Woolf

SHENA MACKAY sheds tears for *Owd Bob*

JONATHAN LAW enters the world of Sylvia Townsend Warner

MAGGIE FERGUSSON drops in on *84 Charing Cross Road*

JEREMY LEWIS crosses the bridge with Richard Church

MELISSA HARRISON explores Gilbert White's *Selborne*

SIMON WILLIS goes walking with Robert Walser

C. J. WRIGHT takes a tour round the *Punch* archive

The Royal Society
of Literature

9 September: John Lahr on 'Tennessee Williams and the Out-crying Heart'

5 October: Michael Holroyd and fellow biographers on living the lives of others

7 October: Jonathan Keates, Kwasi Kwarteng, Michael Symmons Roberts and Joanna Trollope ask: 'What's so great about Trollope?'

15 October: Alexandra Harris on writers and the weather (at the National Portrait Gallery)

22 October: Jonathan Coe, Lavinia Greenlaw, Russell Foster and Deborah Levy talk sleep

9 November: Philip Hensher, Adam Mars-Jones and Rose Tremain on the art of the short story

For the timing and venue for each of the above events and for booking information please visit www.rsliterature.org or call 020 7845 4678.